PHinisheD!

PHinisheD!

Writing a Doctoral Dissertation

Tricia M. Mikolon and Cyrus R. Williams III

UNIVERSITY OF THE CUMBERLANDS | REGENT UNIVERSITY

Bassim Hamadeh, CEO and Publisher
Amy Smith, Senior Project Editor
Abbey Hastings, Production Editor
Jess Estrella, Senior Graphic Designer
Kylie Bartolome, Licensing Coordinator
Natalie Piccotti, Director of Marketing
Kassie Graves, Senior Vice President, Editorial
Jamie Giganti, Director of Academic Publishing

Copyright © 2023 by Cognella, Inc. All rights reserved. No part of this publication may be reprinted, reproduced, transmitted, or utilized in any form or by any electronic, mechanical, or other means, now known or hereafter invented, including photocopying, microfilming, and recording, or in any information retrieval system without the written permission of Cognella, Inc. For inquiries regarding permissions, translations, foreign rights, audio rights, and any other forms of reproduction, please contact the Cognella Licensing Department at rights@cognella.com.

Trademark Notice: Product or corporate names may be trademarks or registered trademarks and are used only for identification and explanation without intent to infringe.

Cover image: Copyright © 2021 iStockphoto LP/shiny7777.

Printed in the United States of America

Brief Contents

Preface xii
Acknowledgments xiv

PART I **Foundational Considerations** **1**
    CHAPTER 1   The Dissertation: Demystifying the Process 2
    CHAPTER 2   Choosing a Topic: Conception and Considerations 11

PART II **Beginning the Process** **21**
    CHAPTER 3   An Overview of the Dissertation Process 22
    CHAPTER 4   The Literature Review 32

PART III **Methodology** **43**
    CHAPTER 5   Qualitative Methodology 44
      By Anita M. Pool, PhD, NCC, NCSC

    CHAPTER 6   Quantitative Methodology 65
      By Michell L. Temple, PhD, EdD, CRC, NCC

    CHAPTER 7   Methodology 86
    CHAPTER 8   Dissertation Proposal Preparation 98

PART IV **Data Collection and Beyond** **111**
    CHAPTER 9   Data Collection and Processing 112
    CHAPTER 10 Results 120
    CHAPTER 11 Implications and Conclusion 127
    CHAPTER 12 Final Defense Preparation 132
    CHAPTER 13 Publication and Your Article 141

Glossary 147
Index 154
About the Authors 159
About the Contributors 161

Contents

Preface xii
Acknowledgments xiv

PART I   Foundational Considerations   1

CHAPTER 1   The Dissertation: Demystifying the Process 2
    The Dissertation Process Outlined 2
    Choosing a Topic 3
    Responsibilities of the Doctoral Candidate, Chair, and Committee Members ... 4
        The Dissertation Chair 4
    Choosing Committee Members 5
        Considerations 5
    Choosing a Methodology 6
        Differences Between the Methodologies 6
    Considerations for Your Title Page and Abstract 6
    Summary 7
    Online Resources 7
    References 8
    Worksheet 1.1: Dissertation Seminar Checklist 9

CHAPTER 2   Choosing a Topic: Conception and Considerations 11
    Choosing a Topic 11
    What Do You Want to Know? 12
    Exploring Your Topic 12
    What Has Been Done up to Today? 13
    Where Are the Holes in the Literature? 14
    Narrowing Your Focus 14
    Summary 15
    Online Resources 16
    Helpful Tips 16
    References 16
    Worksheet 2.1: Narrowing Down Your Dissertation Topic 17

PART II   Beginning the Process   21

CHAPTER 3   An Overview of the Dissertation Process 22
    What Is the Dissertation Process? 22
    Need and Significance of the Study 23

Problem and Purpose Statements 24
Developing Your Research Questions 24
Choosing a Methodology: What Are the Differences? 25
Assumptions, Limitations, and Delimitations 25
An Overview of the Literature 26
Population Considerations 27
Operational Definitions: An Introduction 27
Gathering Data 28
Analysis of the Data 28
Additional Considerations From the Start 29
Writing the Results 29
Summary 30
Online Resources 30
References 30
Worksheet 3.1: Annotated Bibliography Example 31

CHAPTER 4 **The Literature Review** 32
Writing a Solid Literature Review 32
Theoretical and Conceptual Frameworks 33
From Seminal Works to the Present 34
Synthesizing the Literature 34
Summary 36
Online Resources 36
References 37
Worksheet 4.1: Literature Review Guidelines 38

PART III **Methodology**   43

CHAPTER 5 **Qualitative Methodology** 44
By Anita M. Pool, PhD, NCC, NCSC

Overview of Qualitative Methodology 44
Goals and Purpose 45
Interpretive Frameworks 46
Types of Qualitative Research and Considerations of Each 46
Phenomenology 47
Case Study 48
Ethnography 49
Grounded Theory 49
Narrative Research 50
Research Design and Rationale 50
Conceptual Framework 50
Discussion of Methodology: Designing a Qualitative Study 51
Research Problem 51
Research Purpose Statement 52
Research Question(s) 53
Data Collection 53
Summary 58
Qualitative Research Resources 58
Case Study Research 58

    Conceptual Frameworks 58
    Data Analysis 59
    Data Collection 59
    Ethnography 59
    Grounded Theory 59
    Interpretative Phenomenological Analysis 59
    Narrative 59
    Phenomenology 59
    Qualitative Dissertations 59
    Qualitative Research Methodology 59
  References 60
  Worksheet 5.1: Qualitative Research Planner 61

CHAPTER 6 Quantitative Methodology 65
  By Michell L. Temple, PhD, EdD, CRC, NCC

  Overview of Quantitative Methodology 65
    Goals and Purpose 66
    Role of Theory and Type of Variables in Quantitative Research 67
  Types of Quantitative Research and Considerations of Each 68
    Research Design Rationale 69
    Experimental Designs 69
    Quasi-Experimental Designs 71
    Nonexperimental (Descriptive) Designs 73
  Discussion of Methodology: Designing a Quantitative Study 74
    Research Problem 75
    Purpose of the Study 75
    Research Questions and Hypotheses 76
  Participants and Sample Size Justification 76
  Instrumentation and Considerations 77
    Types of Instruments 77
    Criteria to Select an Intact Instrument 78
    Describing Instruments 78
  Data Collection Methods 79
    Data Analysis of Measures 79
    Role of the Researcher 79
    Ethical Considerations 80
    Delimitations and Limitations 80
  Summary 80
  Online Resources 81
  References 81
  Worksheet 6.1: Quantitative Research Planner 82

CHAPTER 7 Methodology 86
  Considerations in Implementing Methodology 86
  Necessary Elements of the Methodology Chapter in a Dissertation 87
  Introduction 87
  Research Questions 87
  Hypotheses 88
  Research Questions and Hypotheses 88

  Participant and Sample Size 89
  Instrumentation 89
  Sample and Data Procedures 90
  Statistical Analysis 91
  Ethical Considerations and Issues of Trustworthiness 91
  Summary of the Chapter 92
 Attachments to Include 92
  Call for Participants 92
  Demographics 93
  Informed Consent 93
  Choosing a Platform or Means of Data Collection 94
 Summary 94
 Online Resources 95
 References 95
 Worksheet 7.1: Outline for Writing Research Questions 96

CHAPTER 8 **Dissertation Proposal Preparation** 98
 Preparation of the Proposal 98
 Institutional Review Board Requirements 99
 The Proposal Process 100
  Gaining Approval From Your Chair 100
  Contacting Your Committee Members 101
  Scheduling Considerations 101
  Preparing Your Presentation 101
 The Proposal Day 102
 The Defense and Considerations 103
 After the Successful Defense 104
 Summary 105
 Online Resources 106
 References 106
 Worksheet 8.1: Checklist for the Proposal Process 108
 Worksheet 8.2: Important Items to Include in Your Presentation 109

PART IV   **Data Collection and Beyond**   **111**

CHAPTER 9 **Data Collection and Processing** 112
 Call for Participants 112
 Demographics 112
 Informed Consent 113
 Gathering Data 113
 Processing the Data 113
 Summary 114
 Online Resources 114
 Worksheet 9.1: Example of Qualitative Results 116

CHAPTER 10 **Results** 120
 Presenting the Data Analysis 120
  Qualitative Data Analysis Presentation 120
  Quantitative Data Analysis Presentation 121

    Notes on Formatting ... 122
    Considerations for the Presentation of Results ... 122
    Summary ... 122
    Online Resources ... 123
    References ... 123
    Worksheet 10.1: Qualitative Research Considerations ... 124
    Worksheet 10.2: Quantitative Considerations ... 125

CHAPTER 11 Implications and Conclusion ... 127
    Writing Your Final Chapter ... 127
    Discussion of Findings ... 127
    Implications for the Profession ... 128
    Strengths and Limitations of the Study ... 128
    Suggestions for Future Research ... 128
    Conclusion of Your Dissertation ... 128
    Summary ... 129
    Online Resources ... 130
    Worksheet 11.1: Checklist for Writing the Final Chapter of Your Dissertation 131

CHAPTER 12 Final Defense Preparation ... 132
    The Final Defense Process ... 132
    Contacting Your Committee Members ... 132
    Scheduling Considerations ... 133
    Preparing Your Presentation ... 133
    The Final Defense Day ... 134
    The Final Defense and Considerations ... 134
    After the Successful Defense ... 135
    Summary ... 136
    Online Resources ... 136
    Reference ... 137
    Worksheet 12.1: Checklist for the Final Defense Process ... 138
    Worksheet 12.2: Important Items to Include in Your Presentation ... 139

CHAPTER 13 Publication and Your Article ... 141
    After Your Dissertation ... 141
    Publication of Your Dissertation ... 141
    Transitioning Your Dissertation to an Article ... 142
    Submitting Your Article for Publication ... 143
    Summary ... 144
    Online Resources ... 144
    References ... 145
    Worksheet 13.1: Exploring Professional Journals for Publication Checklist ... 146

Glossary ... 147
Index ... 154
About the Authors ... 159
About the Contributors ... 161

Preface

The word *dissertation* brings with it numerous connotations, ranging from a major accomplishment to a challenging experience. Such a significant project that serves to earn our PhD as well as to introduce us to academia, the dissertation brings with it excitement, unsureness, and sometimes even dread. The dissertation appears to be a huge project, for which we are handed a guide from the institution, but how does one really go about writing it? The authors have gone through this process as students, committee members, and chairs, and we realize the range of emotions and experiences associated with the entire process. We have traveled this journey with numerous students and always find students craving more information and guidance. Although we were able to find great resources for the philosophical aspects of writing the dissertation and other resources that provide wonderful practical advice, the authors couldn't find one resource that provided both simultaneously.

Our own dissertation chairs and committee members provided us with much-needed guidance and suggestions, and this information was invaluable in successfully navigating the whole project. For us, it seemed selfish to keep these gems of knowledge to ourselves, or only share them with those select students whose committees we served on. Having worked together in the past, we continued to discuss the dissertations we were working on and the struggles of students, and how we helped them transition from student to researcher. Writing a dissertation requires a paradox shift for the student, they must transition from reporting and citing information to synthesizing and adding to the literature. At the same time the student must credit the source all while allowing the literature, data and results to keep its initial meaning and integrity

From our experiences and numerous discussions, the authors decided to create **PH***inishe***D**! *Writing a Doctoral Dissertation* to assist doctoral candidates through this phase of their educational journey. Our goals are to assist the dissertation student in understanding the rigors of writing as well as provide practical information, suggestions, and advice from our combined experience. We have brought in methodological experts on both qualitative and quantitative methodologies to provide you with an overview of important aspects of each. These chapters are not intended to replace your research methodology classes, but instead to enhance your application of that material to your dissertation writing. The authors share a strong passion for dissertations, but more accurately they are passionate about the process of professional development the doctoral candidate goes through, from student to researcher to academic professional.

While this book provides you, the reader, with a great resource, it won't answer every question you have while writing your dissertation. That's what your chair and committee members are for. However, **PH***inishe***D**! *Writing a Doctoral Dissertation* will provide you with a firm foundation rooted in both practical suggestions and a rigorous review of the entire process, from the inception of your idea; through your literature view, proposal, research and data analysis; and to the final defense. It is our hope that you find this book both an academic resource and a means of normalizing your experiences during the dissertation process. You're not alone, although at times it may feel that way. **PH*inishe*D!** is here for you when questions arise or when self-doubt creeps in.

A closing helpful tip to keep in mind from one of my former students, Timothy "Neil" Richey, PhD, sums up the process well:

Dissertation T.I.P.

T-ime (take time to write, and make time to play)

I-nvite (bring people into your circle for support)

P-ersevere (this is just a season and a new one is right around the corner)

These thoughts, combined with the support of your committee and the useful information from **PH*inishe*D!**, will help you navigate the dissertation process successfully, celebrate each step along the way and emerge with not only a new title but with the confidence in yourself and your new role as faculty, scholar, and mentor.

Acknowledgments

The authors would like to thank the contributing authors, Anita M. Pool, PhD, NCC, NCSC, and Michell L. Temple, PhD, EdD, CRC, NCC, for their hard work and dedication to this project. Your insights and expertise in the methodology chapters is priceless. We would also like to thank Abbey Hastings, Amy Smith, Kassie Graves and the Cognella team for your support and encouragement throughout this process.

Tricia M. Mikolon

Thank you as always to my parents, Emil and Patricia Mikolon, and my nephew, E. J. Mikolon, for their undying support and encouragement. Thank you as well to Amy Talipski, Debra Perez, and Sarah Littlebear for your never-ending support, encouragement, and laughs, and to my in-laws James and Darlene Hanson, for always being supportive of my endeavors. And to my co-author, Cyrus Williams, for being first my mentor and now my writing partner. Also, much appreciation to Drs. Kimberly Hardy and Whitney Peay for their great examples and allowing me to use them, and to Dr. Timothy "Neil" Richey for his insightful quote. Finally, I thank my husband Frank A. Levai, Jr., whose love, support, and encouragement are as amazing as he is.

Cyrus Williams

I want to thank my former mentor and now superstar faculty member and author for carrying me throughout this project. I also want to recognize and appreciate my wife and kids for adjusting and supporting me as I wrote, worked and saw clients during this season. I cannot do any of this without my wife Saranette's leadership and support. Finally, I want to acknowledge Regent University, the senior leadership specifically for granting me sabbatical so I could focus on this project and others.

PART I

Foundational Considerations

CHAPTER 1

The Dissertation

Demystifying the Process

The dissertation process may elicit feelings of excitement combined with confusion and unsureness. This is an exciting step in your educational journey and need not be one of mystery. Exploring the dissertation process provides insight into the various phases of the study's development, implementation, and dissemination of results. This chapter will introduce you to the dissertation process and outline the expectations for each phase as well the roles and responsibilities of committee members.

The Dissertation Process Outlined

Each university will have a different format of the dissertation, but the overall process tends to follow a set pattern of development, implementation, and reporting of results. The start of this process is usually contingent on the passing of a **doctoral comprehensive examination**. The contents of this exam and its format will be determined by your institution, but the purpose of the doctoral comprehensive examination is to establish that you have successfully transitioned from doctoral student to doctoral candidate and are able to conduct research independently. The comprehensive examinations are designed to establish your ability to synthesize the various core areas of your field and comprehensively explain them in both written and oral formats. Once you have obtained a passing score, you are then promoted to doctoral candidate. Congratulations on this accomplishment, which should be celebrated as it indicates supervisor-level comprehension of the fundamental knowledge base of your field.

Upon completion of this, you will enroll in the first of your dissertation courses. Often titled "Dissertation Seminar," this course is designed to assist students in developing their research topics and defining their **methodology**, as well as developing the first few chapters of their dissertation. These chapters generally obtain an overview of the project followed by an exhaustive literature review, leading to the current study's research questions. The third chapter outlines the methodology in detail, preparing the student for their dissertation proposal. Each of these chapters is outlined in this book, with Chapter 3 focusing on the overview of your project, Chapter 4 on the literature review, and Chapters 5, 6, and 7 providing a detailed discussion of the methodology. The dissertation committee will also be formed and finalized during this period.

The dissertation proposal will occur at the end of this phase of development and consists of the first three chapters of your dissertation. Your proposal will provide an overview of your study, its purpose and research questions, as well as a review of the literature upon which your study is based. You will also outline your methodology in detail and answer any questions your committee may have. Once you have successfully proposed, a process outlined in Chapter 8 of this book, you will then complete an **institutional review board (IRB)** application to be submitted for approval.

Only after having gained IRB approval can, you enter the next phase of your dissertation: data collection. It is important to keep in mind, should any significant changes in your study take place after you have gained IRB approval, you will need to gain further approval for these amendments. This is a process you will explore with your chair by reviewing your institutional dissertation handbook.

This phase of your dissertation process is characterized by implementing your study. During this time, you will collect and analyz your data and write your final chapters. Often dissertation chapter 4 focuses on reporting your results, and chapter 5 will focus on implications of your research.

When collecting your data, you will need to ensure the confidentiality of your participants as well as the secure management of the date from collection, through analysis, and after you have defended your dissertation. This process is outlined in detail in Chapter 9 of this book. You will focus on analyzing your data and may need to involve a statistician during this phase of your quantitative study to verify your results. Regardless of methodology, your results will need to be written clearly and reviewed by your chair and committee members prior to your final defense. The writing of your results is outlined in Chapter 10 of this text, and the completion of your dissertation chapter 5, where you discuss the implications of your study and provide the conclusion to it, is outlined in Chapter 11 of this book.

Once you have completed writing your chapters and have gained feedback from your chair and committee members, you are prepared to defend your dissertation. Refer to your dissertation handbook for clarification on the process to prepare for this, as well as discuss it with your chair. In general, you will provide your committee with a copy of your finalized dissertation with time to review prior to your defense date, usually at least 2 weeks. You will prepare a presentation of your study, not only with an overview of your study but with a focus on the results and implications/conclusions. As with your proposal, you need to be prepared to discuss all data and findings and answer any questions your committee may pose. The final defense process is explored in detail in Chapter 12 of this text. Publication of your dissertation, transitioning your dissertation to an article, and submitting your article for publication rounds out the dissertation process, and each is discussed in Chapter 13 of this text.

Choosing a Topic

The choice of your dissertation topic will be one that you will need to consider with care. You will spend a significant amount of time researching this topic and discussing it with your chair. It will need to hold your interest but more importantly add original research regarding your profession. It will need to be a thorough and complete research study but one that can be completed within a realistic timeframe given your pending completion of your PhD program, which will act as your introduction to your field as a professional academic.

Your topic may transform as you explore the previous research completed on it. You will narrow your focus and develop your theoretic approach and methodology to pursue the answers to your research questions. This process will be discussed in detail in the following chapter of this book.

Your research into your topic will formulate the literature review of your dissertation. You will explore each topic, building from the seminal works through the significant changes and advancements to the current literature, which will serve as the foundation of your study. Chapter 4 in this book with assist you in understanding this process more.

Responsibilities of the Doctoral Candidate, Chair, and Committee Members

You will have many responsibilities throughout the dissertation process to keep track of. It is important for you to fully explore these as they are defined in your dissertation handbook. In general, it will be your responsibility to work with your chair to form your committee, develop your chapters in accordance with your dissertation handbook while incorporating feedback from your chair and committee members, and maintain open communication with your chair on your project status. Additionally, you will be responsible for developing your proposal, successfully completing research-related trainings (such as the CITI training for human subject protection), completing your IRB application, and gaining IRB approval. You will also need to develop your final defense presentations and successfully defend your dissertation. Your chair and committee will play an important role in supporting and guiding you throughout this process.

The dissertation committee will ideally consist of your chair, a methodologist, and a subject matter expert reader. Additionally, a statistician may be added, as needed. Your dissertation chair may be chosen or assigned by your program. Your committee will help guide you through the dissertation process as well as design and implement your research. Since your dissertation is your first introduction academically to your field, this is a decision not to be taken lightly. Choosing your chair is an important decision with many considerations.

The Dissertation Chair

It is important to understand the role your chair will take in your dissertation process. You will work closely with your chair for advisement throughout the process, and the first thing you will work on together is selecting your remaining committee members. Your chair will provide feedback on your study through its development, as well as help you to move through the process by meeting various deadlines. Your chair will assist you in ensuring your methodology matches your research questions. Your chair will ensure that your research is both ethical and scientifically sound, that research participants are not harmed, and that your data collection and analysis are precise. The chair also assists in refining your writing within your field's professional writing style and preparing you for your proposal and final defense. In some programs the chair will also need to approve your chapter versions prior to you forwarding them to your committee for review.

The chair plays an important role in both guiding you and shaping your study. When choosing someone to request to be your chair, consider someone who has an interest in your topic as well as a strong understanding of your chosen methodology. Also, consider their working style and how it matches your own. Are they quick to return feedback or will you be waiting a few weeks for it? Will they have the ability to meet with you regularly or more sporadically? Does their communication style and frequency match your own?

Once you have decided on someone to approach about being your chair, you need to be prepared. Some potential chairs expect an overview of your project, including a discussion of your research questions, your methodology, your population, and a preliminary explanation of the justification of your study. Some chairs will make their decision rooted in their methodology matching yours, others based on topic, and yet others on their current dissertation and course load, and the time they will need to dedicate to you is significant. Be prepared to propose your study to your potential chair, and if you find a match celebrate! If not, continue to explore other faculty members who may better match your work style and study design.

Most often your chair will need to approve your other committee members, so having them in mind when you meet with your chair is important. You will want to find committee members who are skillful in their role as well as work well together with your chair. The dissertation process involves a lot of moving parts; having a committee that works well together reduces delays and frustration in the future.

Choosing Committee Members

As discussed previously, your chair and your committee will assist you throughout the dissertation process. Choosing your committee members will be based on their qualifications to fit the roles outlined as well as their comfort with those roles and their availability. Your committee members will play a role in shaping your dissertation and guiding your progression through the process, so special consideration of their role and other factors is important.

Considerations

The methodologist will be a faculty member skilled in qualitative or quantitative methodologies, or both. The methodologist will assist you in designing your study and developing your research questions. It is important that your questions match your methodology, so their expertise will be very useful. Most significantly, your methodologist will help in completing your dissertations chapters 3 (methodology) and 4 (results), ensuring that these chapters are clearly written and presented.

Your methodologist will work with your chair in discussing any concerns about your methodology as well as assisting you to resolve any related issues. The methodologist will also assist you in the analysis phase of your dissertation process, although they may request you have a statistician to verify your quantitative results depending on their comfort with statistics. As with choosing a chair, you will want to consider the same aspects of their personality, work and feedback style, and how well these fit with both your chair's and your own styles.

The subject matter expert/reader will assist you in developing your dissertation topic as well as ensuring your literature review is thorough yet concise and includes all significant details. Their experience and insights from the field will make the scaffolding of the literature both strong and logical as it leads to your current study. This committee member will also communicate with your chair any concerns regarding your literature review and possible missing aspects of this in your study, as well as directly with you to assist you in correcting any concerns. As you will be working with them, and they with you and your chair, consideration of their working and feedback style are important as you want to try to form a well-rounded committee that works like a well-oiled machine.

Choosing a Methodology

Methodology is determined by what a researcher is exploring. Ultimately the research questions will determine the methodology. While qualitative methodology explores the lived experiences of individuals, quantitative methodology explores statistical relationships between variables.

Differences Between the Methodologies

If you are exploring the lived experiences of individuals and seek to understand their perceptions, emotions, or thoughts, then qualitative methodology would best fit your study. It uses words to paint a picture of an experience and may use interviews, case studies, or focus groups to gather the data (Creswell & Poth, 2016; Lowhorn, 2007; Reswick, 1994). Open-ended questions are carefully constructed to access the desired perceptions or experiences from the participants. Qualitative research involves smaller population numbers but a longer timeframe to analyze the data. Chapter 5 of this book provides a detailed review of this methodology and its uses.

If you are exploring the relationship between variables using numbers and statistics, then quantitative methodology would best fit into your research design. Quantitative methodology uses surveys or instruments to test or confirm theories or assumptions and to quantify and generalize results to a larger population (Bloomfield & Fisher, 2019; Lowhorn, 2007; Reswick, 1994). This methodology involves larger participant numbers determined by statistical significance and may take more time to gather the data but less time to analyze it. This methodology is discussed in detail in Chapter 6 of this book.

Mixed methodology involves exploring the relationship of variables of quantitative research and the personal perceptions or experiences of qualitative research (Creswell, 2003). It involves a great understanding of the application of each methodology and is much more time-consuming than either methodology used individually. Dissertation students often do not use mixed methodology for these reasons.

Considerations for Your Title Page and Abstract

When developing the title for your dissertation consider if it is descriptive of your study. Can the reader surmise what the research is about from the title? Do the keywords highlight the key issues and variables of the study? Is your methodology, population, and chosen field evident from reading only the title? You want to include each of these aspects in your title yet be frugal with your words. Professional writing styles may vary on title length, so be sure to check your writing manual.

Publishing and copyrighting your work are not always necessitated by a doctoral program. If considering publishing your completed dissertation, which is outlined in Chapter 13 of this text, considering the decision to copyright will arise. Is it necessary to copyright your published work? The answer is no, but registration increases your rights in several ways. For instance, registration is required before a copyright infringement suit can be filed by the creator of the work, and registration creates the possibility for enhanced statutory damages. If you want to go further to protect your copyright, you can register your work with the U.S. Copyright Office for a small fee.

The abstract is written to provide highlights of your study. You want to draw attention to your research problem, the importance and purpose of the study, as well as your theoretical/conceptual framework. Summarize the key research questions as well as significant results, conclusions, and recommendations. Each professional writing style has a limit for the word maximum of an abstract, so be sure to consult your professional writing manual for details. The use of keywords can help capture a reader's attention to important aspects of your study.

Summary

Approaching the dissertation process can be overwhelming due to the unknown aspects of the process. This chapter outlined the process of writing a dissertation and discussed important aspects of consideration when choosing your topic, committee members, and methodology. Development of your title, copyright consideration, and necessary elements of your abstract were also discussed. This chapter provided an overview of this book as well, which will walk you through the dissertation process step by step in each of the following chapters.

Chapter 2 will explore choosing a topic, Chapter 3 the writing of the dissertation overview, and the literature review in Chapter 4. Chapters 5 and 6 explore qualitative and quantitative methods, respectively, while Chapter 7 discusses the writing of the dissertation section on methodology. Chapter 8 brings together the first phase of the process with a discussion of the proposal and gaining IRB approval.

In Chapter 9 data collection and processing are outlined, while Chapter 10 provides a discussion of how to write your results. Chapter 11 walks the researcher through exploring the implications of your study, and the final defense is explored and outlined in Chapter 12. Finally, Chapter 13 discusses what happens after your final defense and the process of publishing your dissertation and transforming it into an article. And in each step of this process **PHinisheD! Writing a Doctoral Dissertation** is with you to provide you with helpful information and practical advice, coupled with a rigorous review of the information. In no time at all, the dissertation process will be demystified, and you'll be on your way to your PhD.

Online Resources

Askanydifference.com: https://askanydifference.com/difference-between-paradigm-and-theory/

A great summary of the differences between paradigm and theory in research.

Doctoral Student Experience (DSE), Dissertation Center, Chapter 1, Problem Statements: https://ncu.libguides.com/c.php?g=1006886&p=7294692

Provides an overview of the considerations in writing a through problem statement for research.

Editage Insights: https://www.editage.com/insights/the-basics-of-writing-a-statement-of-the-problem-for-your-research-proposal

Provides an overview how to effectively write a problem statemen for research studies.

Graduate Research Methods in Social Work: https://pressbooks.rampages.us/msw-research/chapter/7-theory-and-paradigm/

Provides a summary of the differences between theory and paradigm, with learning objectives and exercises to test your comprehension of the topics.

Research.com, How to Write a Research Question: Types, Steps, and Examples: https://research.com/research/how-to-write-a-research-question

Provides a detailed outline of steps to write a complete research question; considering methodology and appropriate examples are provided.

Sciencing.com: https://sciencing.com/differences-between-concepts-theories-paradigms-8415723.html

Provides a review of the differences of paradigms and theories as they apply to research.

Scribbr.com: Research Methods: Definitions, Types, and Examples: https://www.scribbr.com/category/methodology/

Discusses qualitative and quantitative methodology as well as mixed-method design. Highlights the appropriate use of each in research.

Volchok, E. (2015). Measurement and Measurement Scales: http://media.acc.qcc.cuny.edu/faculty/volchok/Measurement_Volchok/Measurement_Volchok3.html

Provides a review of observation, variables, and measurements, as well as a quiz to check your comprehension.

References

Bloomfield, J., & Fisher, M. J. (2019). Quantitative research design. *Journal of the Australasian Rehabilitation Nurses Association, 22*(2), 27–30.

Creswell, J. W. (2003). A framework for design. *Research Design: Qualitative, Quantitative, and Mixed Methods Approaches,* 9–11.

Creswell, J. W., & Poth, C. N. (2016). *Qualitative inquiry and research design: Choosing among five approaches.* SAGE.

Lowhorn, G. L. (2007, May 28). *Qualitative and quantitative research: How to choose the best design* [Presentation]. Academic Business World International Conference. Nashville, Tennessee.

Reswick, J. B. (1994). What constitutes valid research? Qualitative vs. quantitative research. *Journal of Rehabilitation Research and Development, 31*(2), vii–ix.

Worksheet 1.1: Dissertation Seminar Checklist

Topic:
Methodology:
Working Title:

MARKER	DATE COMPLETED
Successfully passed comprehensive examination *or* Successfully gained approval to being dissertation	
Obtained chair	
Finalized dissertation committee • Subject matter expert/reader • Methodologist • Statistician (as needed)	
Gained approval on chapter 1 from chair	
Gained approval of chapter 2 from chair	
Gained approval of chapter 3 from chair	
Gained approval from chair to forward chapters 1–3 plus appendices to committee for initial review	
Incorporated feedback from committee into chapters 1–3 plus appendices	
Scheduled proposal date	
Sent finalized copies of chapters 1–3 plus appendices to committee for review at least 2 weeks prior to proposal	
Developed proposal presentation	
Gained approval of proposal presentation from chair	
Practiced proposal within time limits per dissertation handbook	
Successfully proposed • Incorporated all feedback into proposal chapters	
Completed IRB required training per dissertation handbook	
Completed IRB application	
Gained approval from chair to submit IRB application	
Submitted IRB application	
Gained IRB approval	

(continued)

MARKER	DATE COMPLETED
Collected data in accordance with proposal	
Analyzed data in accordance with methodology	
Wrote results chapter • Submitted to chair for approval	
Wrote implications/conclusion chapter • Submitted to chair for approval	
Gained approval from chair to forward chapters 1–5 plus appendices to committee for initial review	
Incorporated feedback from committee into chapters 1–5 plus appendices	
Scheduled defense date	
Sent finalized copies of chapters 1–5 plus appendices to committee for review at least 2 weeks prior to proposal	
Developed final defense presentation	
Gained approval of final defense presentation from chair	
Practiced final defense within time limits per dissertation handbook	
Successfully defended! • Incorporated all feedback into proposal chapters	
Submitted final chapters and paperwork for graduation	
Submitted final dissertation version for publication	
Adapted dissertation to article for publication	

… CHAPTER 2

Choosing a Topic
Conception and Considerations

Doctoral candidates often enter their first meeting with their chair with lots of ideas of what they want to accomplish in their dissertation. Topics that interest them are intertwined with concepts they have been exposed to in classes or read about in others' dissertations. These can be grand ideas, since often there is the belief that these are what dissertations are made of.

Reality, however, has a slightly different plan. Dissertation topics need to be the next logical step in the literature, following up where others have left off. They also need to contribute to your chosen field, so a PhD in counseling education and supervision would focus on a topic in the counseling field; one in theology would lie within that field of study. Your chosen field is one you are already interested in, so keeping your focus in this field helps with both choosing and narrowing your topic focus.

Too often students need assistance from their chair in narrowing down the focus of their project. Dissertations are meant to enhance the field by adding original research to the field, taking research one step further than it has been taken previously and (something often overlooked) completing it in a realistic time frame for a dissertation course. As a student of mine, Neil Richey, quotes me often as saying, "I had what Dr. Mikolon called a three-book project, but I needed to focus on only the first book for dissertation." According to the Harvard University Graduate School of Arts and Science (2012), "A good dissertation topic: Something that will allow you to produce a polished piece of work within a limited amount of time and with a limited amount of cost."

Choosing a Topic
Picking your dissertation topic can be a challenge, especially as a doctoral candidate with many interests in your chosen field. The first step is picking a topic you are passionate about. Choose something that you find interesting and will continue to for the next year and half or more while you write your dissertation, but also a topic you will continue to want to explore

well past the date your degree is conferred. Your topic needs to be something you want to explore, a topic that will add to the knowledge to your chosen field and aid others in learning more about it.

It also needs to be something you can continue to explore throughout your career. How does this topic fit into your field of study? How will additional work in this topic further understanding within your field? Working smarter not harder is a key here, so choosing a topic you have some experience or basic knowledge of helps tremendously, as you won't be starting from scratch and learning your topic from the ground up. Consider too, this topic may turn into additional studies (those second and third books and beyond), which can help fuel your academic career for years to come.

What Do You Want to Know?

The dissertation process starts with self-exploration. Where do your interests fall in the field? Where do your experiences and knowledge fall in the field? This will help you with the first step of picking a topic within your field.

What aspect of this topic draws your attention and why? How will further study of this topic enhance your understanding as well as that of other professionals in the field? How does this topic relate to your field in general? Is it a niche of the field only a few professionals will explore or study? In this case, what has been done to date on this topic? Or is it an overarching topic that has numerous facets? Which aspect of it do you find most interesting and why? What detail of this aspect intrigues you? Regardless of the topic's pinpoint focus or broad application to the field, picking one or two of these and considering how they relate or possible enhance each other helps you to narrow your focus.

Exploring Your Topic

You've decided on a topic. The next step is to explore exactly what it is you want to know about that topic. What it is that you want to know will help you to narrow your focus, consider **variables** of your study, and determine your methodology. Your topic helps to shape your study, so focus on what you want to know within your chosen field. This will help you to explore it more in depth and discover what the next logical step in the research is.

The first step is to begin exploring the literature. Explore via your university's library database and start with the general topic you are interested in. Make an appointment to meet with a librarian to assist you in starting your research. Begin to gather the research that is already done, from the seminal work to current day, and save copies of each article or book. Then read: Read each article and note what interests you. What variables have been combined within this topic to explore how they relate or interact? Taking detailed notes by completing an electronic bibliography at this time will be helpful throughout the process. Keep a list of the keywords you explored and the number of results from each. This will assist you in understanding to what degree the topic has been explored, as well as the valuable information to include in your literature review later when you write it.

Consider what the next logical step in the previously done research is. As you read articles, make notes of where the findings have left off. Dissertations are original research, but keep in mind enhancing and moving forward the prior literature is original research. What other variables may be considered? Is there another theoretic lens this could be explored through? Exploring these options will help you to narrow your focus and begin to formulate a clearer picture of what it is you want to study and how you want to do that.

Although it may seem tedious at this point, making an electronic annotated bibliography containing the correctly cited article in the writing style of your field will eliminate this process later. The American Psychological Association (APA) is often used for the social science, business, and nursing, while the Modern Language Association (MLA) is often used for the language, cultural, and literary fields. Double-check with your chair and your dissertation handbook to be sure you start out in the correct writing style to avoid problems with reformatting down the road. Next, create an annotated bibliography by adding a summary of the article or book and highlighting how it fits your topic or differs from it. An annotated bibliography "consists of reference list entries followed by a short description of the work called annotations" (APA, 2020, p. 9). This will allow you to then be able to quickly review one document to retrieve the work you need rather than sift through hundreds of actual articles or book chapters. Numerous online resources are available to guide you in the development of your annotated bibliography, as noted in the Online Resources section at the end of this chapter.

What Has Been Done up to Today?

Your topic has been chosen, and after consideration you have chosen variables A and B. What does the literature say about these variables? This may not always be clearly stated or may not be contained in a comparison discussion of the topic or related directly to your field of study. You will need to begin to search for information related to your topic and variables, which may be from other fields.

Consider the topic of burnout. There is a lot of literature about this topic as it relates to first responders, be it nurses, medical professionals, law enforcement, or emergency management services. And what of resilience as a means of managing burnout? But perhaps the literature is sparce, or even nonexistent about burnout and/or resilience and how it relates to educational providers or performers. Where do you begin?

The first step is to gather all the information you can on the topic, in this example burnout. Which population it relates to is not your focus, but if you stumble across information directly related to your chosen population be sure to mark that and keep it handy. You want to gather information from the seminal works, or those foundational works, that highlight the underpinning of the topic in the field (North Central University Library [NCU], n.d.). Depending on when the information was shared with the field, these articles may be quite old, so be sure to not limit your search results when exploring for seminal works (NCU, n.d.). The seminal works will provide the reader with a fundamental understanding and appreciation of the field and the topic within. Continuing to expand on these works, highlighting the significant advancements from that time to the present, is important to provide an exhaustive literature review.

This process will be explored repeatedly for each variable of your study. In our example, you would explore the variables of burnout, its relationship to various fields, such as first responders, and explore each aspect, noting the similarities or differences. Then the focus would shift to your chosen field and specific variable, in our example resilience and educational providers or entertainers. As you complete this process for identifying each variable, you continue to narrow the focus of your topic and explore where the holes in the literature reside.

Where Are the Holes in the Literature?

As the literature review develops, you will notice holes in the literature, or spots where there is no direct link of the topic to your chosen field, population, or variables. This is to be expected and even celebrated, as it indicates that your topic is shining new light on as aspect of your chosen field. Keeping notes of these while developing your literature review, as noted previously, further assists in narrowing your focus to provide solid rationale for your study.

Identifying these gaps in the literature assist in further narrowing the focus of your study and pinpointing the next logical step in the literature. Begin to organize the questions you have about the prior research and how it relates or does not to your variables, methodology, and field of study. These preliminary questions will serve as the draft for your research questions as you continue to narrow the focus of your study.

Narrowing Your Focus

At this time, you find yourself surrounded by piles of documents and an extensive list of articles in your annotated bibliography. You've located the seminal works on the topic and the variables and have noted how they relate to your field. You're building an appreciation of how each variable has formulated and how they inter-relate and differ, noting where in your field they have been addressed before and where mention of them appears absent. You have identified the gaps in the literature and are developing a preliminary sketch of your research questions rooted in your curiosity as to what would fill these holes. So, what's the next step?

You now begin to synthesize your literature on each construct and funnel it to your question. Consider Figure 2.1, where the process begins by shifting from the general information on the topic to the more specific information related to that variable. Here you will begin to discuss the seminal works and acknowledge the information that supports their application to your field and the information on the topic as it relates indirectly to your topic. Synthesis at this level involves putting your voice forward, shifting from reporting what others have done to discussing what has been done while providing a critique of the information as it relates to your topic specifically, noting gaps in the literature not addressed.

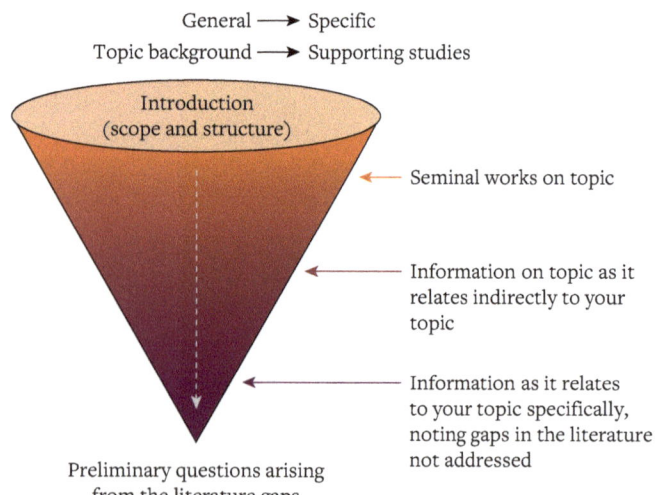

FIGURE 2.1 Narrowing your focus.

Repeat this for each of your major constructs from our prior example (burnout, performers, resilience) following Figure 2.2. You will explore each topic as noted in the first line, then combine each as they relate to each other; in our example that would be burnout and resilience, and burnout and performers. Finally, you further funnel this information to where the three topics intersect or overlap. This is the point where you find the logical next step being the focus of your study. This focus will best be answered by your research questions. Your study now has a focus and preliminary research questions. Congratulations!

You will repeat these focusing steps later when you complete your literature review, so understanding their use now and appreciating the process will assist you further down the road. Investing time now to clarify your study's focus and purpose will provide a solid foundation upon which your research questions and study will be built. You want your foundation to be solid, so spend some time here prior to moving forward and you'll be well rewarded later.

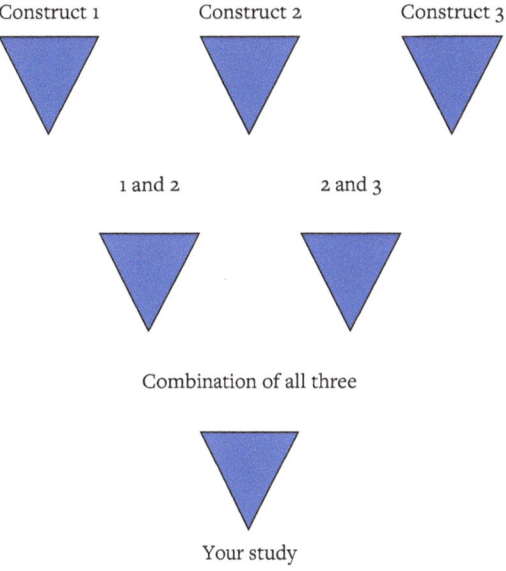

FIGURE 2.2 Focusing steps for the literature review.

Summary

Choosing your dissertation topic is an exciting venture, but one that needs to be considered through a critical lens. This is a topic you will spend a significant time researching and exploring with your chair. It needs to be something that piques your interest but that also adds to your chosen field and on a practical level can be accomplished in a realistic time frame. Work with your chair on narrowing the focus to a manageable timeframe. Although you have many interests and want your introduction into academia to be great, you also want to be able to complete it in a realistic time frame and earn your PhD. Work on the first step now and save the bigger ideas for your career; you'll have a long time to do all you want to accomplish. Remember your dissertation is your first research project, not your last or your greatest

Once you have decided on a broad topic, begin to think about what it is you want to know about it. Is it how the topic can be used in your specific field or with a different population or issue? Start by exploring the literature associated with the topic, field, population, or issue. Remaining open at this early stage of your study's development allows you to consider options that you may not have previously considered. Exploring what has been done and critically evaluating the next logical step in the research process may lead you to the underpinnings of your study. Keeping an annotated bibliography from the start will help you to keep all your hard work organized and easier to manage throughout the process.

Research the seminal works and note any significant changes or contributions over time to the present. Make note of where the topics overlap and where the literature presents gaps as they apply to your field, population, or issue. These gaps can provide insight into areas that require further investigation.

As you begin to narrow your focus, stay on course. Heed the sage advice of "avoid rabbit holes, stay out of the weeds," meaning once you have begun narrowing your focus stay on track. Many interesting ideas and concepts may interest you, but how do they relate to your study's focus? Consider if they are directly related, and if so pursue them. If they are indirectly related, note them for further consideration later in the process. You'll always be able to use them later in chapter 5 of your dissertation when you discuss the next steps of research, so it's not time wasted.

Spending time at this stage of the dissertation process will provide you with both a strong foundation upon which to build your study but a keen focus on what it is your study will contribute to the field and why this contribution is important. These underpinnings of the dissertation will provide the structure upon which the rest of your dissertation will form as well as guide your theoretic approach and methodology. Investment at this stage may appear minimally significant, but you will see the rewards of it later in the process, and later is not that far away.

Online Resources

Bibliography.com: Annotated Bibliography Examples & Step-by-Step Writing Guide: https://www.bibliography.com/examples/annotated-bibliography-writing-guide-with-examples/

> *Provides a step-by-step guide to writing an annotated bibliography as well as structural examples for reference.*

Cornell University Library: How to Prepare an Annotated Bibliography: The Annotated Bibliography: https://guides.library.cornell.edu/annotatedbibliography

> *Provides a description of how to prepare and write an annotated bibliography.*

North Central University Library: Finding Seminal Works: https://ncu.libguides.com/researchprocess/seminalworks

> *Contains a helpful video workshop on how to find seminal works.*

Owl at Purdue: How to Write an Annotated Bibliography: https://owl.purdue.edu/owl/general_writing/common_writing_assignments/annotated_bibliographies/annotated_bibliography_samples.html

> *Outlines the process of writing an annotated bibliography.*

Helpful Tips

1. Clarify your study's focus and purpose early on to provide a solid foundation.

References

American Psychological Association. (2020). *Publications manual of the American Psychological Association* (7th ed.). Author.

Harvard University, Graduate School of Arts and Science (2012, January 27). *How to pick a dissertation topic*. https://gsas.harvard.edu/news/stories/how-pick-dissertation-topic

North Central University Library. (n.d.). *Finding seminal works*. https://ncu.libguides.com/researchprocess/seminalworks

Worksheet 2.1: Narrowing Down Your Dissertation Topic

Following is a list of questions to assist you in narrowing your dissertation topic. Take time to consider each question and note your initial thoughts as you go through each stage of the process. Then come back and assess the value of each as you progress through the initial research phase, finally reviewing it for a third time and formulating your final decision on each aspect.

QUESTIONS	INITIAL THOUGHTS/ ASSESSMENT	THOUGHTS/ ASSESSMENT AFTER INITIAL RESEARCH REVIEW	FINALIZED ASSESSMENT
How does this topic fit into your field of study?			
How will additional work in this topic further the understanding within your field?			
Where do your interests fall in the field? Where do your experiences and knowledge fall in the field?			
What aspect of this topic draws your attention and why?			
How will further study of this topic enhance your understanding as well as that of other professionals in the field?			
How does this topic relate to your field in general?			
Is it a niche of the field only a few professionals will explore or study?			
What has been done to date on this topic?			

(continued)

QUESTIONS	INITIAL THOUGHTS/ ASSESSMENT	THOUGHTS/ ASSESSMENT AFTER INITIAL RESEARCH REVIEW	FINALIZED ASSESSMENT
Is it an overarching topic that has numerous facets?			
Which aspect of the topic do you find most interesting and why?			
Are there assessments to address this issue?			
What detail of this aspect intrigues you?			
What variables have been combined within this topic to explore how they relate or interact?			
What other variables may be considered?			
Is there another theoretic lens this could be explored through?			
What does the literature say about these variables?			
How does the literature address each construct or variable?			
Why is the topic important?			
Who is the audience?			
What is your hypothesis (if appropriate)?			
Where are the gaps in the literature for each construct or variable?			

(continued)

QUESTIONS	INITIAL THOUGHTS/ ASSESSMENT	THOUGHTS/ ASSESSMENT AFTER INITIAL RESEARCH REVIEW	FINALIZED ASSESSMENT
What would be needed to fill these gaps? How would you approach this?			

Credit

Fig. 2.1: Source: Adapted from https://canvas.hull.ac.uk/courses/779/pages/writing-the-review.

PART II

Beginning the Process

CHAPTER 3

An Overview of the Dissertation Process

Understanding the dissertation process is a process within itself. You will find helpful hints throughout this text, but honestly you will only fully understand it once you have come out on the other side having successfully completed it. Let's explore the process and what is involved in the first chapter of your dissertation.

What Is the Dissertation Process?

You will begin the dissertation process officially by starting to write your first chapter. Keep in mind that the dissertation chapter 1 is a highlight of what is to come. You will briefly discuss the background and overview of your study, the needs and significance, as well as your problem and significance statements. Chapter 1 of the dissertation also provides an overview of the methodology and research questions, but each of these elements will be discussed in greater detail in chapter 2 and included in chapter 3 as applicable.

The worksheet provided in Chapter 1 outlines the steps of the dissertation process. By now you have successfully passed comprehensive examination or successfully gained approval to begin dissertation, whichever the process is at your institution. You have obtained a chair by following the steps and guidelines provided in Chapter 2 and have finalized your dissertation committee, securing a faculty member to serve as your subject matter expert/reader and methodologist, as well as a statistician, as needed. You will then begin to work on writing chapter 1 of your dissertation, which we will explore in detail here.

You will work through a process of gaining approval on chapters 1, 2, and 3 from your chair as well as any appendices, and then have them all reviewed by your committee members. After incorporating feedback into your documents, you will then schedule your proposal date. Two weeks prior, in general, you will provide the finalized copies to your committee for their review. During this time, you will develop your proposal presentation, gaining approval on it from your chair and practicing, practicing, practicing!

Once you have successfully proposed, you will incorporate all feedback into your proposal chapters 1–3 and the associated appendices and complete the IRB required training per the dissertation handbook and the IRB application. Once you have gained approval from your chair to submit IRB application, you will submit it and await the IRB's approval. Once IRB approval has been granted, you will begin collecting data in accordance with the proposal and then move to the analysis of the data in accordance with methodology.

Next comes more writing, now focusing on the completion of your results chapter, which you will submit to your chair for approval and then work on writing your implications/conclusion chapter. Upon gaining approval from your chair on the final chapters and all appendices, you will forward these to your committee for their initial review. Once again, you will incorporate all feedback from the committee into chapters 1–5 of the dissertation plus the appendices and then schedule your final defense date!

Next you will send the finalized copies of chapters 1–5 plus appendices to your committee for review at least 2 weeks prior to proposal, develop the final defense presentation, gain approval of this presentation from chair and practice, practice, practice your final defense within time limits per dissertation handbook. Then you defense day arrives! This is a process we will explore in depth in upcoming chapters. Once you have successfully defended, you will once again incorporate all feedback into proposal chapters, submit your final chapters and paperwork for graduation, and, if required by your program, submit your final dissertation version for publication and work on adapting your dissertation to an article for publication. Even if these last two steps are not required by your program, they are highly recommended and will be outlined in coming chapters. You've worked tremendously hard on this dissertation, so don't stop now! Continue with publications and presentations related to it! You've got this!

For now, let's begin to explore the contents of your first chapter of your dissertation. It will begin with an overview of the background and study. Here you will provide a brief overview of the literature leading to your question as well as an overview of the major sections of the chapter, which are outlined next. Finally, you will wrap up with a summary of the need for this study. Keep in mind that as you write this chapter you want to capture the reader's attention, making them want to read more!

Need and Significance of the Study

In these sections you will outline the need and significance of your study. You will start with the *need for the study*, calling on current literature to provide the rationale for your study. Sell your study here, making it clear why it's important by rooting it in the literature. This is where you point out the "holes" in the literature and highlight the need for your study and how it will fill the gaps in and advance research to the next logical step. Also, stress how it will benefit the field and stakeholders, for example counseling, counselors, or counselor educators or supervisors.

Then move onto the *significance of the study*. Here you will discuss the topic of your research, the importance and value of your study, and the impact this will have on the field and key stakeholders. Provide a summary of the literature related to the topic, as you will expand on this in the second chapter of your dissertation dedicated just to that topic and bring the literature logically to the questions you have and plan to explore in your study. Once again, discuss the gaps or holes in the literature that led to your questions, rooting your study in the existing literature and displaying how your study will further the research in this area.

Problem and Purpose Statements

The next sections you will explore are both the problem and purpose statements. You will start with exploring your **problem statement** by clearly stating your research problem and providing literature to support the current issue and its importance to your field. Then provide a summary of the literature as it applies to the problem within recent times, usually defined as within the last 5–7 years, including the seminal works, and building up to today as explored in Chapter 2 of this book. Be sure to identify the gaps in the literature that your study aims to fill, highlighting the connection between your study and the current literature once more.

Next you will outline your **purpose statement**. Here you will clearly articulate the specific purpose of the study. Keep in mind that your purpose statement needs to flow logically from the need for the study. It is a good idea to briefly discuss your intended methodology at this point as well, alerting the reader to exactly how you plan to access and process the data.

Discussing the **research paradigm** is important at this juncture. "A research paradigm is a model or approach to research that is considered the standard by a substantial number of researchers in the field based on having been both verified and practiced for a long period of time" (Editages.com, n.d.). Explain to the reader the objective of your study, in the sense of will it compare, explore, or describe the phenomena? Discuss the focus of your study and what this study will add to the field—and most importantly how you are going to do that.

Developing Your Research Questions

Developing your **research questions** is an important step in the development of a research study. You will want to identify the theory or theories and provide the origin or source. Concisely state the major theoretical propositions and/or major hypotheses with a reference to a more detailed explanation in chapter 2 of your document. Discuss the theory and how it relates to your research questions and chosen approach. These include your overarching questions, which you will provide a copy of with your interview questions in your appendices in chapter 3 of your dissertation.

Quantitative studies will contain research questions along with hypotheses for each. You will provide your research questions (RQ) and the **hypothesis** of what you believe the results will be based on the most recent literature. Once you have your results you will share them in chapter 4 of your dissertation. Even if your hypothesis is incorrect, don't worry. These results are often the most interesting as they challenge the expected and reveal new insights. This methodology will be explored more in Chapter 6 of this book, with a detailed discussion of research questions related to it.

For qualitative studies, your research questions do not contain hypotheses. The research questions for this methodology usually start with "how" or "what" but not "why". For example, "How do parents influence the counseling of children?" or "What impact does stress have on teacher efficiency?" This methodology is explored in detail in Chapter 5 of this book and explores all considerations, including the research question formatting.

Choosing a Methodology: What Are the Differences?

As mentioned previously, qualitative methodology is explored in detail in Chapter 5 of this book while quantitative methodology is discussed in Chapter 6. In this chapter, as in your writing of your first dissertation chapter, we will highlight these in regard to decision-making at this point in the study development. As part of this discussion, you will consider your theoretic framework and the nature of the study. You will also provide an overview of your study's population, recruitment of participants, and data analysis.

The **theoretic framework** explores the foundational concepts and phenomenon of your study. Here you will aim to concisely summarize the conceptual framework derived from the literature, again what you will explore in detail the second chapter of your dissertation. You want to connect the framework to your study's key elements, approach, research questions, and data analysis and let the reader know you will be exploring this in detail in chapter 2. Provide a summary of the lens you are using to look at the data and consider where the different theories overlap, that is, the lens you are viewing your study and data through. This concept is explored in depth in the next chapter of this text.

The **nature of the study** is the discussion your chosen design and the rationale for this choice. In this section you will summarize the key concepts of the study and concisely present the methodology. You want to be sure to include a description of who your population is and how you will collect the data. Keep in mind, the easier the collection for the participants the more likely they are to follow through. Along this line of thinking, keep times realistically. Think about if you were to participate in a study; up to an hour is manageable for most, but more time may discourage participation on your behalf or for others.

How will you analyze the data? Briefly summarize it here, keeping in mind that you will go into detail on the literary support in chapter 2 and discuss it in detail in chapter 3 of your dissertation document. Finally, include a summary of how you will complete your initial analysis and how you will code the data for qualitative studies. Discuss any self-analysis you will use, such as bracketing, journaling, memos, and the like, and if you have any external reviewers, either people or programs, as well as how you will refine your themes. Again, each of these steps is outlined in Chapters 5 and 6 of this book as they explore qualitative and quantitative methodologies in detail.

Assumptions, Limitations, and Delimitations

It is important to explore your own beliefs with research, as well as the limitations and delimitations. **Assumptions** are basically what you believe to be true but can't support with the prior literature/science. You want to be sure to discuss only those relevant to the study and how these assumptions guide or impact the study. These may be rooted in your prior experience, your worldview, or your culture. Discussing these increases your trustworthiness as a researcher, which allows the reader to understand what you bring with you into the researcher role, and, more importantly, as will be discussed in a later section, how you will manage these to ensure objectivity throughout the research process.

You will next turn your discussion to **the scope and delimitations**. In this section you will discuss the specific focus of your questions and why you chose them, providing an explanation of why they are important to the field. Then you will discuss your population with attention to who will be included and who will be excluded and an explanation of why. Discuss the focus and frameworks of the study, explaining how they relate to the study and any areas they won't address or that you chose to exclude along with the reasoning for your decisions. Finally, discuss the potential generalization of the results, focusing on who can benefit from this study's results in addition to the obvious stakeholders of the field.

When exploring the **limitations** of your study, discuss the restrictions of the design and methodology, with attention to aspects such as dependability, generalization, and the like. Include a discussion of any personal biases you have that may impact the study and how you will manage/overcome them.

Complete this section of your chapter by highlighting once more the significance of your study. Briefly address how this study will advance your field and what specific areas or stakeholders it will impact. Keep in mind, this needs to align with the problems the study is focusing on.

An Overview of the Literature

In this section, you provide an overview of the literature. Chapter 2 of your dissertation is where you allow the research to build the foundation for your study. There you will explore each of aspect of your study in detail, grounding it in the literature and citing your sources for nearly all of this chapter. Allow the research to do the work for this chapter; your assumptions and goals were outlined in chapter 1 and will be revisited in chapters 3 and beyond.

Keep your focus on what's already out there and how it funnels from the seminal works throughout the history of the research to today and how this logically leads to your questions.

For now, you will focus on providing a **literature search summary** and a brief overview of the literature related to your topic, just enough to highlight the seminal work, the significant changes or advancements over time, and the current literature. This will then logically display the gaps in the literature that your study aims to address. Keep in mind this is just an overview; chapter 2 of your dissertation will go into an exhaustive review of the literature as outlined in this book's next chapter.

When writing your literature search summary be sure to discuss how you completed your literature search. What library databases or search engines did you use? What terms, or combination of terms, did you search? You can include more detailed search terms in an appendix if it's an extensive list.

If the literature was limited on a topic or how it applied to your specific population, how did you address this? Did you expand your search to relevant fields? For example, perhaps you explored the topics of first responders and medical staff if exploring burnout for correctional officers as they may experience similar types of events and subsequently similar burnout.

Consider how the literature on the topic, regardless of population or theory, applies to your topic. How does the specific literature relate to your topic, population, and/or theory? What gaps are there? Consider what connections were not made and in which areas. Is your summary concise yet thorough? It need not be exhaustive at this point; that will happen in the chapter dedicated to the literature review. But you want to ensure that it goes from the seminal works to the present and logically leads to your current questions.

When you are completing this overview, you are most likely simultaneously writing or at least outlining your literature review. Consider the following steps while you do this to ensure you don't miss any pertinent information: Did you explore each construct/phenomenon through the discussion of the seminal works and how they addressed the problem? Did you do the same for your methodology? Does your literature review, through time to the present, address how each study addressed the problem? Creating an **annotated bibliography** can be a very useful step at this time in preparation for writing your full literature review.

Use the literature to support your chosen methodology and how you are conceptualizing each variable. Synthesize all the literature on each construct and funnel it to your question. Then repeat this for each major variable. Marry these together to lead the reader to your question.

Explain why this approach is the most appropriate at this time and how it will lead to meaningful contributions to the field. This process is outlined in detail in Chapter 4 of this text. The discussion here is just for consideration as you work on your current literature overview. Remember, work smarter not harder!

Population Considerations

When you discuss your study's population, you are providing an overview at this time. You have taken time to develop your demographics, which clearly identify the qualifications or roles your subjects will need to participate in your study and have made this as specific as possible to increase replicability, so be sure to explain this information here. Explain how you have taken steps to ensure that you only include demographic information you specifically need for you study; for example, if gender is not a variable of consideration, don't ask it. If graduating from a CACREP program is, ask their school, program, and year of graduation so you can verify it. Explain what reasons there are to not include a participant in your study such as if you know them personally.

Discuss how you will handle if a participant declines to answer questions or does not complete the interview, or if they contact you later and ask not to be included. Hopefully these things won't happen, but planning is the best prevention and preparation for these events. Finally, provide a review of your informed consent and the IRB necessary information, referring the readers to the associated appendices.

Operational Definitions: An Introduction

Operational definitions are the explanations of your study's variables. Consider this the recipe for your study to increase replicability. How do you define each variable? For example, are you using anxiety's definition according to the DSM-V or are you using something else? Clear operational definitions allow understanding and make replication possible.

Provide operational definitions for your study in your own or other authors' words, whichever you are using, but cite these to be clear and avoid plagiarism. Each variable needs to be defined specifically to your study to provide clarification for the reader. Be careful not to overgeneralize; use this opportunity to define your research variables and constructs. Keep in mind that each of these will need to be addressed in the literature in chapter 2 of your dissertation, so that's a helpful guide to determine what needs to be defined and what doesn't.

Another important consideration is that all variables in your demographics need to be operationally defined for your study, and each needs to be pertinent to your study to use it. You cannot simply collect information regarding the subjects if it is not directly related to your study. This is an important component of research ethics, the goal of the researcher is to strive to reduce bias by collecting only relevant data acknowledging relevant differences what exist in variables (APA, 2020).

Also "be sensitive to labels" (APA, 2020, p. 133). Be sure to avoid bias and be careful to avoid comparisons in which "false hierarchies" (APA, 2020, p. 134) may be present. Finally, consider variables that may bring about bias, such as age, ability, racial or ethnic group, and gender or gender identity, to name a few. Collecting data that is directly related to the research questions will help reduce bias and prevent crossing personal boundaries with your subjects.

Gathering Data

Gathering data is an important aspect of research. Future chapters on qualitative and quantitative methodologies, Chapters 5 and 6, respectively, and Chapter 9 in this book will explore this topic in depth. In the first chapter of your dissertation, you will provide an overview of your data collection methods. You will address your role as a researcher, how data is collected, and how it will be stored.

You also want to explain your own biases and perceptions and how these influence your research, and more importantly how these biases will be managed to allow you to manage the data objectively. Clarifying what, if any, your relationship will be with the participants is important, as you don't want to influence their participation or their responses. Ethical considerations, such as incentives, are also be discussed here along with how these will be managed.

In the dissertation, you will collect your own data. How this will be accomplished and in what manner will be outlined briefly here and explored in more detail in your dissertation's third chapter. Where will you reach out to participants? Will you use electronic mailing lists or other established mailing lists, or will you use another platform? Be specific here and include an appendix if necessary to outline the details. The management of the data and its storage will also be highlighted here and expanded on later in your methodology chapter.

Keep in mind that the easier it is for the participant to complete the demographics and informed consent the more likely they are to participate in the study. You want to limit the number of contacts and meetings to what is necessary. Consider the timeframe as many participants are less likely to invest in over an hour, and determine if follow-ups are truly necessary? Explore this from the participants' point of view. Would you be likely to participate in your study? Why or why not? The "why nots" may give you insights into barriers for your participants.

Analysis of the Data

The fourth chapter of your dissertation will explore the analysis of your data and results. But in the first chapter you provide an overview of this process. You want to discuss the instruments you use. These include your call for participants, the demographic questionnaire, the informed consent, and your interview protocol for qualitative studies. Explain your choice of videoconferencing platform, how you will store any recordings or artifacts, and what data storage system or devices you will use and how they will be locked, thereby protecting the confidentiality of the participants.

Discuss how data will be destroyed after the mandated IRB timeframe and what data destruction systems will be used. Using a professional system is more trustworthy than stating you will delete information or destroy the USB you stored it on. Explain the data analysis systems you will use, if applicable. For each of these elements, clarify if you published or produced them and discuss the reasoning for your decision to use each, commenting on such aspects as efficiency, cost, ease of use, and the like, and how these enhance the analysis.

If you are using published instruments, you want to include the creator/author, date of publication, population norms, validity, and reliability. If creating your own instrument, you need to explain the literature you based it on as well as provide the content validity and justification for its use versus other well-established instruments. This will all be explored in more detail in Chapter 9 of this book.

You also include the IRB approval number upon gaining it. At this juncture, you simply note that you have completed any required trainings, for instance the CITI training, and note that you will be applying for IRB approval upon your successful proposal. After your proposal is approved, you will change your first three chapters from future tense, or what you are proposing to do, to past tense, as your final dissertation will be in the past tense, explaining what you did. Don't worry, this will make more sense as you progress through the dissertation process.

Additional Considerations From the Start

Your first chapter will also include a reference to many documents you will include as appendices for your first three chapters. You will create an informed consent, IRB approval documents, and any related ethical research training. You want to summarize the protective measure for human subjects you plan to use as well as those to protect confidentiality.

Think ahead as you are developing your study. Consider the worst-case scenarios and prepare for them now, thereby reducing the need to go back to the IRB for additional approval for any changes you need to make later down the road. These issues may include participant withdrawal or removal, data collection, analysis, storage, and destruction methods or other ethical issues such as power differentials or personal relationships with participants.

Explore the internal validity or the credibility and external validity or transferability, dependability, and confirmability, as well as intra-intercoder reliability if applicable. Exploring each of these and considering how they apply to your study or may present themselves is important, as you want to consider each possibility prior to presenting your proposal to your committee. Once the IRB has approved it, you need to submit an amendment. Although this process is not difficult, it is time-consuming and avoidable through due diligence and consideration of these different elements from inception of your study. Each of these are discussed in more detail as they arise in each chapter of your dissertation. At present they are simply provided for your consideration and awareness.

Writing the Results

You won't write results until after you have collected all your data and completed your analysis. This process is outlined in Chapter 10 of this book, and for both qualitative and quantitative methodologies in Chapters 5 and 6. For consideration, when writing your results, consider the format dictated by your methodology. Chapter 10 of this book provides checklists for each methodology to assist in ensuring consistency when writing your results.

Summary

Although the dissertation process can be overwhelming when you first start, taking it step by step will allow each part to make sense, and soon you will be able to envision how they connect. In the first chapter of your dissertation, you introduce your reader to the problem and purpose statements of your study. An overview of your literature review, which is expanded on in your second chapter, is provided to display how your study will advance understanding and fill in any gaps from the past that lead to your research questions. Your operational definitions will provide a clear recipe for your variables while your chosen research methodology will be outlined to explain how you will gather and analyze your data. *PHinisheD! Writing a Doctoral Dissertation* will be with you every step of the way.

Chapter 1 of your dissertation provides an overview of your study, much like this chapter did of the process. Each subsequent chapter of your dissertation will focus on specific details of your study, including the literature review, the methodology, the data analysis and results, and finally the implications of your study for your field and consideration for future research. Coming chapters will explore each aspect of the dissertation chapters in more detail to assist in both your preparation and the writing of them.

Online Resources

Moon, K., & Blackman, D. (2017). *A guide to ontology, epistemology, and philosophical perspectives for interdisciplinary researchers.* https://i2insights.org/2017/05/02/philosophy-for-interdisciplinarity/

Provides a great summary of ontology and epistemology and how they relate to research.

Purdue University. (n.d.). *Purdue Online Writing Lab: Writing a literature review.* https://owl.purdue.edu/owl/research_and_citation/conducting_research/writing_a_literature_review.html

Provides a great summary of how to write a literature review with helpful hints.

Research.com. (n.d.). *How to write a research question: Types, steps, and examples.* https://research.com/research/how-to-write-a-research-question

Provides an overview of research questions and an exploration of how to develop these with pertinent examples.

Royal Literary Fund. (n.d.). *Resources: The structure of the literature review.* https://www.rlf.org.uk/resources/the-structure-of-a-literature-review/

Provides a review of how to structure a literature review and hints for exploring literature.

References

American Psychological Association. (2020). *Publications manual of the American Psychological Association* (7th ed.). Author.

Editages.com. (n.d.). *Question and answer forum: Planning to write.* https://www.editage.com/insights/how-do-i-make-a-research-paradigm#:~:text=A%20research%20paradigm%20is%20a,a%20long%20period%20of%20time

Worksheet 3.1: Annotated Bibliography Example

Mikolon, T. M., & William, C. (2022). *PHinisheD! Writing a doctoral dissertation*. Cognella.

Individual institutions provide handbooks that outline the dissertation format for their students. This book aims to assist both instructors and students throughout the dissertation process by providing an overview of the structure, elements, and science involved regardless of field of study. It provides an essential guide to the dissertation process, from inception of the topic through completion of the literature review; from methodology considerations to an overview of data analysis, providing helpful suggestions in each area and cumulative step. This text is unique in that it explores the dissertation process objectively without focus on one education field, providing sound support to both educators and students as they advance through the dissertation undertaking.

CHAPTER 4

The Literature Review

The literature review is where you allow the research to build the foundation for your study. You will explore each of aspect of your study in detail, grounding it in the literature and citing your sources for nearly all this chapter. Allow the research to do the work for this chapter; your assumptions and goals were outlined in chapter 1 and will be revisited in chapters 3 and beyond. Keep your focus on what's already out there and how it funnels from the seminal works, throughout the history of the research to today, and how leads to your questions.

Writing a Solid Literature Review

In writing your literature review, you want to follow your institutional dissertation manual or guidebook. Most universities have the literature review in chapter 2, where you provide a thorough discussion of the literature related to your topic from the foundational works throughout history to today.

The literature review starts with an introduction. Here you want to begin by briefly restating the problem and purpose, then provide a brief overview of the literature to support these.

At this point, the literature review is brief and supports your problem and purpose statements. Provide the reader an overview of the prior works that have led to your problem and purpose statements. Then provide a highlight of the sections of the chapter, ensuring a preview sentence or two of each. For instance, this chapter explores the theoretic foundation of your study, so a few sentences explaining what that is and its importance in your study would be provided here.

Consider your primary and secondary readers when you provide the overview. Consider your theoretic foundation once again. An introductory overview may be stated as "constructivist and professional identity theories will provide the theoretic foundation upon which this study is built and will guide the research design as well as analyze the data." In the introduction you provide the highlights of the study thus far as well as a preview of the coming sections of the current chapter.

Theoretical and Conceptual Frameworks

A PhD is a doctor of philosophy. Given this, the dissertation's focus on theory is important as it provides the philosophical underpinnings of your study. Your **theoretic framework or lens** can be defined as

> Theoretical frameworks provide a particular perspective, or lens, through which to examine a topic. There are many different lenses, such as psychological theories, social theories, organizational theories, and economic theories, which may be used to define concepts and explain phenomena. (North Central University Library [NCU], n.d., para 1)

Your theoretic lens will provide the reader with an explanation and understanding of theoretic framework upon which you are building your study topic and analyzing your data.

For example, when you have an eye exam the ophthalmologist provides an initial lens for you to view. They then add an additional lens on top to check for better clarity. A way to visual your theoretic lens is to consider how each theory overlaps, and where they come together provides the clearest view theoretically through which you will view your variables, build your study and analyze the data, as presented in Figure 4.1.

Figure 4.1 provides a visual of how theories overlap to form your lens.

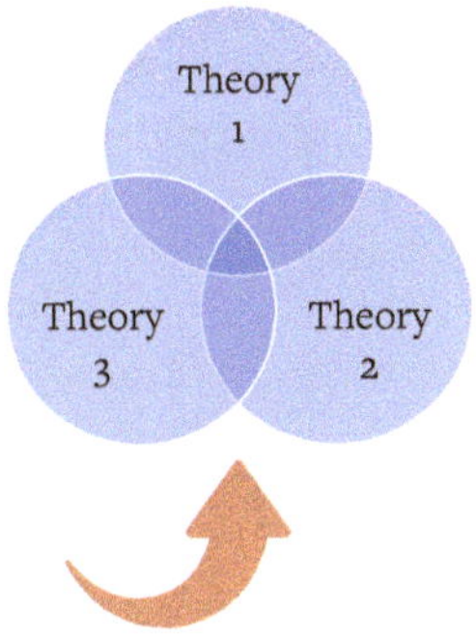

However, theories will overlap and not necessarily fully combine, leading to more questions of how they interrelate and impact each other (Niederman & Salvatore, 2019). The explanation of how you operationally view this lens is key. Like other definitions provided in your introductory chapter, you will need to **operationally define** your theoretic lens for the reader at this point in your literature review. Providing a thorough review of each theory's origin, major tenets, and how each matches or delineates from your study is important. Discussing each theory from the seminal works to today, noting any significant changes or developments, will assist in this process. What innovations were added? How do these apply to your study? Cite these consistently to provide the theoretic framework.

FIGURE 4.1 Your theoretic lens.

Discuss why you chose this theory and how it fits the scope of your study? How will it explore your research questions and add to the field? How will it challenge the application of the theory or expand its use? Are you using this theory with a new population or problem?

Your discussion of a conceptual framework will apply if you are completing a qualitative research design. Keep in mind your theoretic framework is the lens you will be processing the data through; your conceptual framework is your approach to your study. When discussing your conceptual framework, use the literature to explore each of the concepts or phenomena of your study. What's already been done? What did prior researchers find? Outline your framework through the literature and include key terms and definitions for each according to the literature. Consider how these relate to each other. How do they relate to your study? How were they previously applied to the problem? What will be different if your application of this theory is applied to this problem?

From Seminal Works to the Present

The literature review starts with a summary of your literature search, which was briefly touched on in Chapter 2. Discuss how you completed your literature search for your research. As discussed previously, keep a list of the keywords you explored and the number of results from each when initially exploring your topic. What library databases or search engines did you use? What terms (or combination of terms) did you search? You can include more detailed search terms in an appendix if it's an extensive list. If the literature was limited on a topic or how it applied to your specific population, how did you address this? Did you expand your search to relevant fields?

Literature reviews are expected to be an exhaustive review of all relevant literature from the seminal work to the present. To accomplish this, you need to explore the literature as it compares directly and indirectly to your variables and chosen theoretic/conceptual frameworks. Explore each construct/phenomenon by discussing the seminal works and how they addressed the problem. Discuss your chosen methodology and use the literature to support it and how you are conceptualizing each variable. Synthesize all the literature on each construct and funnel it to your question. Then repeat this process for each major variable and element of your study, meaning your theoretic or conceptual framework as your methodology. Bring these topics together and outline their connections to lead the reader to your research question. Explain why this approach is the most appropriate at this time and how it will lead to meaningful contributions to the field.

Synthesizing the Literature

"Synthesize the literature" is something every doctoral candidate hears at some point in their dissertation process, and most likely during the literature review. But what does it mean to synthesize the literature? The Oxford Learner's Dictionary (n.d.) defines synthesis as "the act of combining separate ideas, beliefs, styles, etc., a mixture or combination of ideas, beliefs, styles, etc." Synthesizing the literature, then, involves comparing the findings of prior research studies, leading to your study variables and techniques. It entails exploring the seminal works to provide the foundational explanation of each topic, then systematically moving throughout history from the seminal works to today, highlighting significant changes or contributions while noting any holes that appear in the literature.

Operational definitions of your variables should also be explored. Think of these as your recipe of your study. To ensure replicability, outlining these in detail exactly as you envision them is important. One person's definition of "a lot of snow" may be a few inches or feet depending on their experiences and perspectives. To eliminate such confusion, providing a concise definition of your theoretic lens, conceptual framework (as applicable), and variables is imperative.

Figure 4.2 may assist in visualizing how to synthesize the literature in your review process. Similar to how you narrowed your focus in Chapter 2, you can adapt this figure to consider your literature synthesis. For each topic, be it your theoretic lens, topic of discussion, or variables, you explore the background information related to the topic, starting at the seminal works and moving throughout history to the present day, noting significant changes or adaptions along the way. You then explore each as they relate more closely to your study, ending up where the literature leads to an aspect directly related to your topic. This will be repeated for each element of your study, thus providing an exhaustive literature review.

Figure 4.3, as previously discussed in Chapter 2, will assist you in further focusing the literature review. You have already discussed each construct in detail and will now walk the reader through how each interrelates. Consider how each element interacts with every other element individually, then combine them all. This process ensures that your literature review is exhaustive and complete, leaving no aspect of your study unexplored.

A final aspect of synthesizing the literature to consider is putting your voice first rather than reporting the finding of prior literature. Putting your voice first simply means that you provide an overview and summary of the literature and how various prior works compare to each other, either supporting or contrasting findings. This is accomplished by paraphrasing and citing prior studies and their findings rather than directly quoting them. This allows the reader to hear your interpretation of the material and experience how you view them fitting together or contradicting each other. This synthesis of the literature is what separates a student from a researcher. Students often report what has already been done by others; researchers explore what has been done by other researchers but combine the prior findings to formulate a more complex thought about how they interrelate. Strive to transition from student to researcher, as this is a fundamental characteristic of someone holding a Doctorate of Philosophy.

Finally, it is recommended that you include a summary of the chapter to assist the reader in transitioning from one chapter to the next. Concisely summarize each theme/construct and discuss what is known/unknown in the literature. Highlight how your study fills in these gaps, then lead to chapter 3 with a sentence or two of how you will explore these gaps.

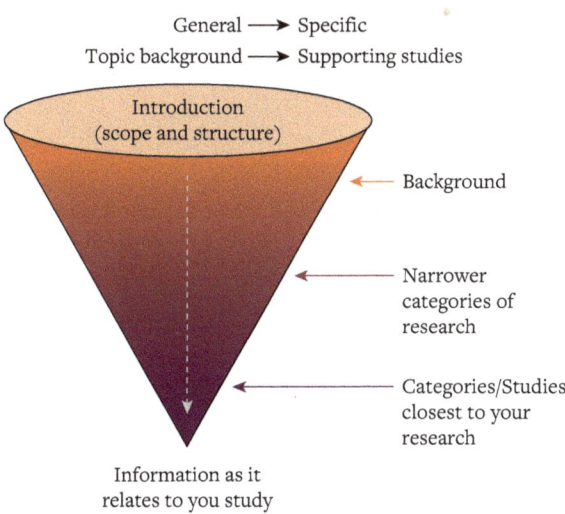

FIGURE 4.2 Structure of a literature review for an article.

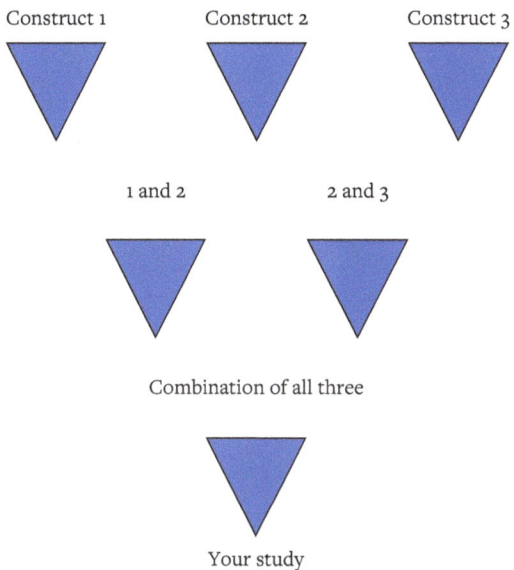

FIGURE 4.3 Focusing steps for the literature review.

Prior to turning in your literature review, read it. Review it for typos and errors, and double-check your grammar and spelling. Can your wording be more concise? Did you read it out loud to check the flow? Although reading it out loud may sound silly, it's very useful to help you evaluate your writing more objectively. Did you correct any spelling or grammar errors? Have you cited all information correctly according to your field of study's preferred writing style? Proofreading your literature review at this point will take time, but it's a good investment to ensure you send the most polished version of your literature review to your chair and/or committee.

Consider submitting your literature review through Grammarly and practice reading it out loud, which help in making sure your writing reflects what you intended to.

Summary

Writing a literature review can be a daunting task when you first approach it. Systematically exploring each element of your study allows you, as the researcher, to outline the scaffolding upon which you are building your study. Pay special attention to the major elements of your study and dissertation. You want to explore the theoretic lens, conceptual framework, and major constructs of the study, providing a thorough review of what has previously been accomplished in each area and exploring how each interrelates.

The literature review provides the opportunity to explain how you came to your research questions while supporting them in the scientific findings of the researchers who came before you. It is also an opportunity to transition from a student to a researcher, moving beyond simply reporting others' findings to synthesizing those findings to provide the foundation upon which your contribution to the field will be laid. Allow the reader to understand your hard work and knowledge by putting your voice first. As a contributing member of your field, your voice matters, and your dissertation is where you first introduce it to your current colleagues and those to come.

Online Resources

Grammarly: www.grammarly.com

A great tool to help proof your writing, including a plagiarism check.

Kramer, L. (2021, September 17). How to write a stellar literature review [Blog post]. *Grammarly Blog.* https://www.grammarly.com/blog/literature-review/?&utm_source=google&utm_medium=cpc&utm_campaign=10273012991&utm_targetid=aud-1114839904227:dsa-1233402314764&gclid=Cj0KCQ-jwqp-LBhDQARIsAO0a6aLYHaAr0uM26_v9tXSYntav9xcgDVgOaCQ4rtu1AW6vmWkzkGW4OaMaAr-11EALw_wcB&gclsrc=aw.ds

Provides an overview and useful suggestions on how to write a literature review.

North Central University Library. (n.d.). *Library how-to guides.* https://ncu.libguides.com/howto

Provides an overview of research methods and design as well as the research process, among other topics.

Purdue Online Writing Lab. (n.d.). *Writing a literature review.* https://owl.purdue.edu/owl/research_and_citation/conducting_research/writing_a_literature_review.html

Discusses when to write a literature review, what to include, and how to format it, among other topics related to the literature review.

University of Guelph, McLaughlin Library. *Seven steps to writing a literature review.* https://guides.lib.uoguelph.ca/c.php?g=130964&p=5000948

This site walks the user through seven steps, from how to narrow your topic to searching for and writing a literature review.

References

Niederman, F., & Salvatore, M. (2019). The "theoretical lens" concept: We all know what it means, but do we all know the same thing? *Communications of the Association for Information Systems, 44,* 1–33. https://doi.org/10.17705/1CAIS.04401

North Central University Library. (n.d.). *Theoretic frameworks.* https://ncu.libguides.com/researchprocess/theoreticalframeworks

Oxford Learner's Dictionary. (n.d.). *Synthesis.* https://www.oxfordlearnersdictionaries.com/us/definition/english/synthesis

Worksheet 4.1: Literature Review Guidelines

Following is a list of questions to assist you in completing your literature review. Take time to consider each construct or variable of your study.

QUESTIONS	NOTES: WAS THIS ACCOMPLISHED FOR EACH CONSTRUCT? WHERE IS THIS SUPPORTED IN YOUR LITERATURE REVIEW?	DATE COMPLETED
Introduction: Does your introduction briefly restate the problem and purpose, providing a brief overview of the literature to support these? Does your introduction highlight the sections of the chapter? (Use this outline as guide.) Did you provide an overview of each section of the chapter?		
Theoretic lens: Did you provide a thorough literature review of the theory from the seminal works up to today? What has changed? Did you note what innovations were added? Did you address how these apply to your study? Did you cite these consistently? Did you thoroughly explain why you chose this theory and how it fits the scope of your study? Did you discuss how you will explore your research questions and add to the field? Did you address how this research challenges the application of the theory or expands its use? Did you consider if it applies to a new population or problem?		

(continued)

QUESTIONS	NOTES: WAS THIS ACCOMPLISHED FOR EACH CONSTRUCT? WHERE IS THIS SUPPORTED IN YOUR LITERATURE REVIEW?	DATE COMPLETED
Conceptual framework (if applicable): Does the conceptual framework apply to your study? If so, did you use the literature to explore each of the concepts or phenomena of your study? Did you discuss what has already been done? Did you discuss prior findings? Did you outline your framework through the literature? Did you include key terms and definitions for each according to the literature? Did you discuss how these relate to each other? Did you discuss how they relate to your study? Did you discuss how were they previously applied to the problem? Did you discuss what will be different if your application of this theory is applied to this problem?		
Have you started at the seminal works? Have you highlighted the major additions to the literature from then to the current time? Have you funneled the literature to highlight the gap your study is going to fill?		

(continued)

QUESTIONS	NOTES: WAS THIS ACCOMPLISHED FOR EACH CONSTRUCT? WHERE IS THIS SUPPORTED IN YOUR LITERATURE REVIEW?	DATE COMPLETED
Did you explore each construct/phenomenon?		
Did you discuss the seminal works and how they addressed the problem?		
Does your literature review move through time to the present? How did they address the problem?		
Did you synthesize all the literature on each construct and funnel it to your question?		
Did you repeat these steps for each major variable?		
Did you unite these to lead the reader to your question?		
Methodology: Did you discuss what methodology is?		
Did you use the literature to support your chosen methodology and how you are conceptualizing each variable?		
Did you explain why this approach is the most appropriate at this time and how it will lead to meaningful contributions to the field?		
Summary: Did you concisely summarize each theme/construct?		
Did you discuss what is known/unknown in the literature?		
Did you discuss how your study fills in these gaps?		
Did you lead to chapter 3 with a sentence or two of how you will explore this/these gaps?		

(continued)

QUESTIONS	NOTES: WAS THIS ACCOMPLISHED FOR EACH CONSTRUCT? WHERE IS THIS SUPPORTED IN YOUR LITERATURE REVIEW?	DATE COMPLETED
References: Did you provide a reference for each work cited in the body of the text? Did you double-check each reference is used in the body of the text?		
Proofreading: Did you review your work to ensure it is concise? Did you read it out loud to check the flow? Did you correct any spelling or grammar errors? Have you cited all information correctly according to your field of study's preferred writing style? Do you have a peer to review the document?		

Credits

Fig. 4.1a: Copyright © 2018 Depositphotos/creativestall.

Fig. 4.2: Source: Adapted from https://canvas.hull.ac.uk/courses/779/pages/writing-the-review.

PART III

Methodology

CHAPTER 5

Qualitative Methodology

By Anita M. Pool, PhD, NCC, NCSC

The choice to conduct a qualitative study for one's dissertation is influenced by several factors, and the most important one is the research question; a qualitative research question can only be answered with qualitative methodology. After you have decided that your research question is best answered by conducting a qualitative study, you need to be equipped with sufficient information from the qualitative literature to design and conduct a methodologically congruent and credible study. Conducting qualitative research can be rewarding yet demanding, and you must be prepared for the time investment involved. What follows is a guide to designing and conducting a solid qualitative study.

Overview of Qualitative Methodology

Qualitative research differs philosophically from quantitative research and has been referred to as "naturalistic" since it takes place in the natural, real-world setting of the participants (Lincoln & Guba, 1985). It is conducted when we want to understand an individual's or group's experience with a **phenomenon**, to discover the interpretation or meaning of an individual's **lived experience**, or if we desire to develop a new theory or add to an existing theory. This contrasts with quantitative research, which is used to determine cause and effect, predict outcomes, or determine relationships between variables (Merriam & Tisdell, 2016).

Essentially, qualitative research involves the use of words as data, whereas quantitative research involves the collection and analysis of numbers (Braun & Clark, 2013).

It is critical to understand the philosophical differences in order to know *why* you are conducting a qualitative study. Unfortunately, as with other qualitative language, little consistency can be found in the literature regarding this aspect of qualitative research. We have chosen to use the terminology of a few select authors for our discussion. According to Creswell and Poth (2018) and Billups (2021), the four philosophical assumptions underpinning qualitative research include **ontology** (the nature or view of reality), **epistemology** (how knowledge is justified and the relationship between the researcher and that being studied), **axiology** (the role of values), and **methodology** (the process and language of research). Thus, qualitative researchers believe the following: Reality is subjective and multiple realities can exist; researchers get as close to participants as possible since they are the primary instrument of data collection; values are part of the research process and the **researcher's "positionality"** is made known to the reader; and qualitative research methods are inductive, emerging, and flexible and are shaped by the researcher (Billups, 2021; Creswell & Poth, 2018).

Scholars have identified the following key characteristics of qualitative research that reflect the four underlying philosophical assumptions. According to Billups (2021), Creswell and Poth (2018), and Merriam and Tisdell (2016), qualitative research

- occurs in the field and the researcher has substantial engagement with participants in the natural, real-world setting;
- has a focus on meaning and understanding;
- includes multiple and unique perspectives and meanings;
- is holistic, complex, reflective, and interpretive;
- involves the researcher as the primary instrument of data collection and analysis;
- utilizes **purposeful sampling** since participants are intentionally selected;
- has an emergent and flexible research design;
- is an inductive process;
- results in rich descriptions of participants and their experiences.

These characteristics make qualitative methodology uniquely different from quantitative methodology and highlight the need for a large investment of time on the part of researcher. If you are undertaking a qualitative study for your dissertation research, you should be prepared for the necessary time investment in order to conduct a well-designed, credible study.

Goals and Purpose

As stated previously, qualitative researchers are interested in understanding individuals' experiences—how they interpret the experiences and the meaning they assign to the experiences, and how they construct their worlds accordingly (Merriam & Tisdell, 2016). Although not an exhaustive list, some possible goals of qualitative research include the following: to understand the world in which participants live and work, to enact societal improvements, to change ways of thinking, to find solutions to real-world problems, to address inequities and to empower people, to convey the voices of individuals who have been suppressed or marginalized, to transform lives, and to address the meaning of inclusion (Creswell & Poth, 2018). According to these authors,

> Qualitative studies not only add to the literature, but they give voice to underrepresented groups; probe a deep understanding of a central phenomenon; and lead to specific outcomes such as stories, the essence of a phenomenon, the generation of a theory, the cultural life of a group, and an in-depth analysis of a case. (p. 130)

In short, qualitative research is conducted when we want to explore or discover something that cannot be understood from numbers alone.

Interpretive Frameworks

The intended goals or outcome of your research may help you determine the **interpretive framework** (sometimes referred to as your **epistemological perspective**) for your study. As mentioned previously, you may desire to simply understand a phenomenon, or you may want to enact change as a result of your research. "Seeking an understanding of the world is different from generating solutions to real-world problems" (Creswell & Poth, 2018, p. 32). As seen in Table 5.1, adapted from Creswell and Poth (2018), various interpretive frameworks and possible researcher goals are provided as guidance for choosing your interpretive framework.

TABLE 5.1 Interpretive Frameworks and Researcher Goals

INTERPRETIVE FRAMEWORK	POSSIBLE RESEARCHER GOALS
Social constructivism	To understand the world in which participants live and work
Transformative	To act for societal improvements
Postmodern perspectives	To change ways of thinking
Pragmatism	To find solutions to real-world problems
Feminist theories	To conduct research that is transformative for women
Critical theory/critical race theory	To address areas of inequities and empower humans
Queer theory	To convey the voices and experiences of individuals who have been suppressed
Disability theories	To address the meaning of inclusion

Note. Adapted from *Qualitative Inquiry & Research Design: Choosing Among Five Approaches* (4th ed., p. 34), by J. W. Creswell & C. N. Poth, 2018, SAGE.

It should be noted that your interpretive framework (or epistemological perspective) is not the same as your **conceptual framework**. However, your interpretive framework is reflected in your conceptual framework and may explicitly include one of the theories mentioned. Conceptual frameworks will be discussed later in this chapter.

Types of Qualitative Research and Considerations of Each

Some researchers choose a general or basic approach to qualitative research; however, specifying a particular **approach to inquiry**, sometimes referred to as a genre or tradition, adds to the quality of the study design and ensures **methodological congruence**. Although all qualitative research shares some basic attributes, as mentioned, each approach to inquiry has a distinct focus and often identifies specific methods of data collection and analysis. Using the appropriate approach is necessary to gain the insights desired from the research questions.

Numerous approaches to qualitative research are presented in the literature. This can be overwhelming for doctoral students attempting to choose the most appropriate qualitative approach for their study. Some of the more common approaches are presented in this chapter to help narrow your focus. McCaslin and Scott (2003) propose a helpful five-question method for determining the appropriate approach or tradition for one's study. Students struggling to decide which approach is best for their study may find this exercise beneficial (Table 5.2).

TABLE 5.2 "Five-Question Method" by McCaslin and Scott (2003)

QUESTION TO DISCOVER PREFERRED APPROACH	ASSOCIATION TRADITION
1. If I could discover the meaning of one person's lived experience, I would ask _____ (individual) about _____.	Biography (narrative)
2. If I could discover the shared lived experiences of one quality or phenomenon in others, I would want to know_____.	Phenomenology
3. If I could experience a different culture by living/observing it, I would choose to experience _____.	Ethnography
4. If I could discover what actually occurred and was experienced in a single lived event, that event would be _____.	Case study
5. If I could discover a theory for a single phenomenon of living as shared by others, I would choose to discover the theory of _____.	Grounded theory

Mark L. McCaslin and Karen W. Scott, Selection from "The Five-Question Method For Framing A Qualitative Research Study," *The Qualitative Report*, vol. 8, no. 3, p. 450. Copyright © 2003 by The Qualitative Report.

It is important to note that just as there are different genres or approaches to qualitative research, there are also different types within each qualitative approach. The different types vary according to their philosophical underpinnings, and the type you choose will depend on the purpose of your research and your research question.

Phenomenology

Phenomenology is a philosophical approach and a genre of qualitative research and is basically the study of experiences. A phenomenological approach to research is chosen when one wants to understand the essence or meaning of participants' lived experiences with a particular phenomenon. The defining characteristic of phenomenology is that it involves the exploration with a group of individuals who have experienced the phenomenon under study, which is typically phrased as a single concept or idea. According to Creswell and Poth (2018), "Phenomenologists focus on describing what all participants have in common as they experience a phenomenon (e.g., grief is universally experienced)" (p. 75). A phenomenological approach is well suited if one is studying emotional or intense human experiences (Merriam & Tisdell, 2016).

Different forms or types of phenomenological research can be used for one's study depending on the intended outcomes of the study and other factors. Various types are presented in the literature; however, they essentially fall within two basic categories: interpretive or descriptive (Lopez & Willis, 2004). The primary differences relate to the focus of each and the role of the researcher. In short, interpretive or hermeneutical phenomenology focuses on the interpretation of participants' experiences, whereas descriptive phenomenology (also referred to as transcendental or psychological phenomenology) focuses on a description of participants' experiences. The process of **epoche**, or **bracketing** of personal experiences with the phenomenon, is part of descriptive or transcendental phenomenology since the goal of the researcher is to achieve transcendental subjectivity (Lopez & Willis, 2004). In essence, the researcher must determine if a description of experiences is desired or if an interpretation of experiences is preferred.

This important distinction will help students to identify the appropriate qualitative approach. Data for phenomenological studies are primarily collected through in-depth participant interviews, although other sources of data may also be collected for example observations, poems, documents, or the like (Creswell & Poth, 2018). Procedures for data analysis will vary according to the type of phenomenological study; therefore, students should follow the recommendations of the chosen approach to ensure methodological congruence.

Interpretative Phenomenological Analysis

According to Smith (2011), interpretative phenomenological analysis (IPA) is a newer approach to phenomenological research and is becoming one of the most used methodologies in psychology. It has become increasingly popular for dissertation research because of its straightforward approach to data collection and data analysis. The theoretical underpinnings of IPA are phenomenology, ideography, and hermeneutics. Due to its idiographic nature, IPA studies typically have smaller sample sizes than other phenomenological studies (Smith et al., 2009). According to Smith (2011), "IPA is concerned with the detailed examination of personal lived experience, the meaning of experience to participants, and how participants make sense of the experience" (p. 9). It is important to note the name of the approach, *interpretative* and not *interpretive*, which is a common mistake seen in textbooks, dissertations, and journal articles. Johnathan Smith is the founder of IPA and Smith et al. (2009) provide detailed guidance for conducting an IPA study.

Case Study

Case study research as a qualitative approach involves the exploration of a case or cases within a contemporary, real-life setting. The case(s) could involve a person, community, process, event, or organization (Creswell & Poth, 2018). According to Yazan (2015), it is one of the most frequently used methodologies; however, emerging researchers are often confused because of a lack of consensus in the literature regarding design and implementation.

As with phenomenology, several different approaches can be taken for case study research, and each differs in terms of how the case or cases are defined, the design of the study, methods of data collection and analysis, and strategies for validation (Yazan, 2015). For example, Merriam (1998) conceives the case(s) as occurring in a bounded context (e.g., program, institution, process, or social unit), whereas Yin (2002) believes that a case does not have clear boundaries between the phenomenon and context; thus, it is particularly helpful for program evaluation. Alternatively, a case is defined as "a complex, functioning thing" with "a boundary and working parts" (Stake, 1995, p. 2), and it is considered more beneficial for studying people or programs and less beneficial for studying events or processes (Yazan, 2015). The three authors also differ in their epistemological perspectives, as well as their approaches to case study design. Furthermore, all three have different recommendations for data collection, data analysis, and validation strategies. Yazan (2015) provides a concise side-by-side comparison of the approaches to case study research, which may be helpful for students who are wondering which approach best suits their research project.

Ethnography

Ethnography is a genre of qualitative research that focuses on human society and culture. An ethnographic approach is taken when one wants to understand a cultural group and the shared beliefs, values, and attitudes that result in behavior patterns for a specific group of people. The patterns can also be described as customary social behaviors, rituals, or regularities (Creswell & Poth, 2018; Merriam & Tisdell, 2016). According to Creswell and Poth (2018), "Ethnographers study the meaning of the behavior, the language, and the interaction among members of the culture-sharing group" (p. 90). It is important to note that the cultural group must have been together long enough for these patterns of behavior to develop (Wolcott, 2008).

Data collection in an ethnographic study involves the researcher being immersed as a participant observer at the site for an extended period of time. Sources of data include formal or informal interviews, as well as the researcher's diary or journal. Additional sources of data may include symbols, artifacts, documents, or photographs. The result of an ethnographic study is a detailed, holistic, thick description of the overall interpretation of the patterns of the group (Creswell & Poth, 2018; Merriam & Tisdell, 2016).

As with the other genres of qualitative research, there are many forms of ethnography. Two of the common forms are realist ethnography and critical ethnography. Realist ethnography involves an objective account of the situation with the researcher remaining in the background. Realist ethnography is typically written from the third-person point of view. On the other hand, critical ethnography includes the researcher from an advocacy perspective and may have a political purpose (Creswell & Poth, 2018). As stated previously, the purpose of the research and the research questions will drive the decision as to which approach to ethnography is most appropriate.

Grounded Theory

Grounded theory is a qualitative design in which the researcher generates a general explanation or theory for a process or action. A grounded theory approach is taken when the researcher wants to create a theory generated from the data rather than using a theory "off the shelf" (Strauss & Corbin, 1998). Thus, the researcher seeks to develop a theory of a process or action, or add to an existing theory, and the result is a "substantive" theory rather than a formal theory. Grounded theory is often used when studying processes, or how something changes over time (Creswell & Poth, 2018; Merriam & Tisdell, 2016). The focus on theory building is what differentiates this approach from other qualitative approaches (Corbin & Strauss, 2015).

Like other qualitative approaches, data for grounded theory studies typically come from interviews; however, observations and documents may also be included as sources of data. In contrast to other qualitative approaches, data collection is guided by theoretical sampling, whereby participants are theoretically chosen to help the researcher develop the theory. After the theory is generated, additional participants may be identified through discriminant sampling, in which the researcher gathers information from different individuals to determine if the theory holds true (Creswell & Poth, 2018).

Although various approaches to grounded theory exist, two popular approaches are Corbin and Strauss's structured approach and Charmaz's constructivist approach. Corbin and Strauss's approach is more systematic, step by step, and involves the constant comparative method of data analysis. Alternately, Charmaz's advocates for a social-constructivist perspective, which is more interpretive and less systematic. Regardless of the approach taken, the result is a substantive-level theory, which may be accompanied by a model (Creswell & Poth, 2018).

Narrative Research

Narrative is a qualitative approach that focuses on the "lived and told stories of individuals" (Creswell & Poth, 2018, p. 67). The stories are sometimes referred to as *life stories* or *life histories*. They may be coconstructed between the participant and researcher, or they emerge through the story told to the researcher (Riessman, 2008). Thus, narrative research has a collaborative feature due to the interaction and dialogue between the participant and researcher. The result of a narrative study is a synthesis of the stories, which are connected chronologically by the researcher. The meaning of the stories is embedded in the larger cultural context since narrative stories occur within specific situations or places (Billups, 2021; Creswell & Poth, 2018). According to Billups (2021), a narrative design may be guided by the question, "What does this story reveal about this individual(s) and his or her (their) world(s)?" (p. 6).

Data for narrative studies are collected primarily through oral storytelling of the participants' lived experiences, and the "text" of the story is the data set that is analyzed (Creswell & Poth, 2018). Although participants' stories are the primary source of data, other forms of data may also be collected and can include things such as journal entries, field notes, observations, documents, and photographs or other artifacts. These additional data sources may expand the researcher's understanding of the participants' stories (Sheperis et al., 2017).

As with the other approaches to qualitative inquiry, various forms of narrative research exist, including autobiography, biography, and oral history, among others. The choice of approach is often guided by the function of the narrative, such as the nature of the experience or the audience for the narrative (Creswell & Poth, 2018). Data analysis strategies vary according to the type of narrative approach that is chosen.

Research Design and Rationale

Conducting sound qualitative research begins with a solidly designed study that includes sufficient support from the qualitative literature for all methodological decisions. Rationale should be provided for the choice of qualitative methodology in general, and also the qualitative approach specifically (e.g., descriptive phenomenology, constructivist grounded theory). The justification should include the reasons the chosen qualitative approach is most suitable for answering the research question.

Conceptual Framework

Conceptual and theoretical frameworks guide all aspects of the study and research process, including the development of research questions, sampling and data collection methods, and data analysis procedures. It is important for graduate students to understand the vital role of conceptual and theoretical frameworks for guiding qualitative research so their studies will be conceptually and methodologically sound (Ravitch & Riggan, 2017). Although the terms *conceptual frameworks* and *theoretical frameworks* are often used interchangeably in the literature, some authors make distinctions between the two. We have chosen to follow the guidance of a few authors who differentiate between the two types of frameworks and advocate for conceptual frameworks as a more comprehensive framework for a qualitative study.

According to Ravitch and Riggan (2017), a strong conceptual framework is a critical component of a well-designed qualitative research study. However, researchers often experience confusion about what a conceptual framework is, why it is important to the overall strength of their study, and how to approach developing one. Without a solid understanding of these key concepts, researchers run the risk of creating proposals that suffer from "overall confusion and lack of coherence" (p. 33).

Ravitch and Riggan (2017) describe a conceptual framework as "the overarching argument for the work—both why it is worth doing and how it should be done" (p. 8). Maxwell (2005) clarifies that it "incorporates pieces that are borrowed from elsewhere, but the structure, the overall coherence, is something that you build, not something that exists ready-made" (p. 41). Accordingly, development of a conceptual framework presents a unique opportunity for the researcher, which is to showcase their command of the literature, their analytical skill, and their capacity for original thought (Bloomberg & Volpe, 2016; Maxwell, 2005).

Even if a researcher understands what a conceptual framework is, developing one that is strong and compelling can be a challenge. Developing a "total, logical orientation and [association] of anything and everything that forms the underlying thinking, structures, plans and practices and implementation of [the] entire research project" is hard to do, especially for novice researchers (Kivunia, 2018, p. 47). There are expected components to a conceptual framework, which include the researcher's personal interests, the researcher's positionality, the topical literature, and the theoretical framework (Ravitch & Riggan, 2017).

When a conceptual framework is utilized for a qualitative study, it provides a "superstructure" for the work (Ravitch & Riggan, 2017). It clearly identifies what is being studied and why it is important in relation to the body of research already in existence. Further, the framework explains the interrelationship of the constructs, variables, and factors being studied and informs the entire study (Miles et al., 2014; Ravitch & Riggan, 2017). It is an iterative process that should begin at the outset of the study and may involve many revisions. It is recommended that a graphic representation of the conceptual framework accompany a narrative of the framework.

Discussion of Methodology: Designing a Qualitative Study

To design a solid qualitative study, you must include all elements of the research design and ensure that adequate detail is provided for each. These include the research problem, purpose statement, research questions, and sampling procedures. Furthermore, all aspects of the research design must align to ensure methodological congruence.

Research Problem

According to Creswell and Poth (2018), designing a methodologically congruent study begins with the identification of the research problem. As the researcher, you will identify the idea or central phenomenon you would like to study and the practical issues that lead to a need for the study. In other words, you provide a compelling argument and strong rationale for studying the issue or topic. The rationale is based on what has already been studied about the topic and exists in the literature. The rationale should also be related to gaps in the current literature.

The research problem (sometimes referred to as the research problem statement) "lays out the logic of the study" (Merriam & Tisdell, 2018, p. 77) and may be conceptualized as a funnel shape, with the broadest aspect of the topic at the top of the funnel and the narrowest at the bottom. In other words, after introducing the reader to the key concepts and what has already been studied about the topic, you will lead your reader the down the funnel to your specific question (Merriam & Tisdell, 2016). It is important to note that "research problem statement" is a misnomer; the research problem is more than simply one statement. It is situated within an opening paragraph or paragraphs of the study and should include the topic to be studied, the research problem, the evidence from the literature about the problem, the deficiencies in the evidence or gaps in the literature, the importance of the problem for certain audiences, and the purpose statement (Creswell & Poth, 2018).

Research Purpose Statement

The research purpose statement provides the primary purpose for the study. It should be written clearly and concisely so the reader does not have to guess the purpose of the study. Creswell and Poth (2018) provide a "script" for writing your research purpose statement:

> The purpose of this _____ (narrative, phenomenological, grounded theory, ethnographic, case) study is to (was? will be?) to _____ (understand? describe? develop? discover?) the _____ (central phenomenon of the study) for _____ (participants) at _____ (the site). At this stage in the research, the _____ (central phenomenon) will be generally defined as _____ (a general definition of the central phenomenon). (p. 132)

The research purpose statement is encoded with language or keywords specific to each qualitative approach. Billups (2021) and Creswell and Poth (2018) provide guidance for aligning the research design, purpose statement, and research questions by encoding proper terminology. See Table 5.3 for examples.

TABLE 5.3 Words for Encoding the Purpose Statement, Research Questions, and Title

NARRATIVE STUDY OF A SINGLE INDIVIDUAL (OR TWO)	PHENOMENOLOGY STUDY OF THE SHARED MEANING/ ESSENCE OF A PHENOMENON	GROUNDED THEORY RESEARCHER GENERATES A THEORY TO EXPLAIN AN ACTION, ITERATION, OR PROCESS	ETHNOGRAPHY STUDY OF A CULTURE-SHARING GROUP (OR INDIVIDUAL FROM A GROUP)	CASE STUDY INVESTIGATION OF "BOUNDED SYSTEMS" WITH A FOCUS ON A CASE OR CASES
Narrative study	Phenomenological study	Ground theory	Ethnography	Case study
Stories	Describe	Generate	Culture-sharing group	Bounded system
Epiphanies	Understand	Develop	Cultural behavior and language	Single or collective case
Lived experiences	Experiences	Propositions	Cultural portrait	Event, process, or program
Chronology	Meaning	Process	Cultural themes	
	Essence	Substantive theory		

Research Question(s)
Research questions guide your study. These include both the central question(s) and sub-questions that will be explored. Careful consideration of the wording of each is essential to tap into the insights and experiences the researcher is hoping to explore.

Central Question
The central research question will be your "grand-tour" question, which will be open-ended and often begins with the words "how" or "what." The central question tells the reader what you are attempting to "discover," "explain," "explore," "identify," or "explain" and may be a restatement of your purpose statement. You want to try to avoid words such as "relate," "influence," impact," "affect," and "cause" since those are associated with quantitative methodology. Creswell and Poth (2018) recommend that researchers reduce the study to one central research question and several sub-questions, whereas Maxwell (2013) suggests that three or four main questions are reasonable. Regardless of the number of research questions, it is important to remember that research questions are not the specific interview questions. Rather, the research questions are the broader questions that guide the study (Merriam & Tisdell, 2016).

Sub-Questions
If you are following the recommendation of Creswell and Poth (2018) and are using a primary question and sub-questions, you want to give careful consideration to your sub-questions, which should further refine or subdivide the central research question into smaller parts. As with the central question, sub-questions should be open-ended and begin with "how" or "what." Creswell and Poth (2018) recommend using a small number of sub-questions.

Data Collection
Considerations for data collection extend beyond simply the types or sources of data to be collected. Creswell and Poth (2018) conceptualize data collection activities as a "circle" and include everything from locating participants to storing data securely (p. 149). Due to the emerging nature of qualitative research, some aspects of data collection may change as the study evolves. Potential ethical issues should be considered throughout data collection and will be discussed at the end of this chapter.

Purposeful Sampling
Sampling in qualitative research is **purposeful sampling** and is sometimes referred to as **purposive sampling**. Through purposeful sampling, participants are intentionally selected who can best provide the most information and insight about the topic under study (Billups, 2021; Creswell & Poth, 2018; Merriam & Tisdell, 2016). In other words, the participants purposefully inform an understanding of the phenomenon under study. Creswell and Poth (2018) propose three considerations involved in purposeful sampling: the participants (or sites); the type of sampling strategy (which varies according to the specific approach), and the size of the sample.

Participants and Sites
Identifying participants and gaining access to the participants or a site are critical considerations in qualitative research. You must first determine the unit of analysis, or the sample, to be studied.

"The researcher thus needs to choose what, where, when, and whom to observe or interview" (Merriam, 2016, p. 96). For some studies, this may be an easy decision. For others, it may require some thought and consideration. The issue of who is best to provide the necessary information to answer the research question will vary depending on the type of qualitative approach. For example, for an ethnographic study, the participants would be members of the culture-sharing group being studied and may all be at the same site. Alternately, a phenomenological study will include individuals who have experienced the phenomenon and may be located at various sites. Attention should also be given to whose perspective is necessary to best address the research question. For example, if you are interested in understanding a marginalized individual's experience with oppression, you do not want or need the perspective of the oppressor.

An additional consideration is the possibility that the researcher may need permission or approval to gain access to certain sites or individuals. In this case, the researcher must first go through a gatekeeper to gain access (e.g., an administrator, a community leader, etc.) before **participant recruitment** can begin. Participant recruitment involves the procedures that will be used to solicit or invite potential participants to participate in the study. These procedures could involve activities such as distributing flyers advertising the study, sending emails to electronic mailing lists, or sharing the invitation through professional contacts or organizations. Some researchers may choose to solicit participants through social media due to its popularity and far reach; however, Gelinas et al. (2017) caution researchers to be mindful of the potential ethical issues that may arise from using social media as a means of locating and contacting participants. It is important to note that IRB approval must occur before any participant recruitment can begin, regardless of the chosen recruitment strategies.

Types of Sampling Strategies

Various types of sampling strategies can be found in the qualitative literature, including strategies such as **criterion sampling**, convenience sampling, **snowball sampling**, and homogenous sampling, to name a few. Some studies may utilize more than one sampling strategy, and the decision as to which sampling strategy or strategies to use may be based on the approach of the study. For example, criterion sampling is commonly used for phenomenological studies since the participants must meet certain criteria (e.g., experience with the phenomenon, a particular age, certain race or ethnic identity, etc.) and may also utilize snowball sampling, whereby participants may recommend other individuals they know who have had experience with the phenomenon. Be sure to follow the guidance and recommendations of the experts for your chosen approach, as some sampling strategies are specific to certain approaches (e.g., theoretical sampling for grounded theory).

Sample Size Justification

Due to the nature of qualitative research, qualitative studies typically utilize smaller sample sizes that quantitative studies. The exact number of participants or sites necessary for a study is not a predetermined number, although some general recommendations can be found in the literature for specific approaches. For example, one or two participants are appropriate for narrative studies, and 20–30 participants (or more) are recommended for grounded theory studies. However, great variation in participant number recommendations can be found in the literature for phenomenological studies. Ultimately, you will need an adequate number of participants to answer your research question. Lincoln and Guba (1985) propose that one collects data to the point of saturation, or when no new information or insights are gained from participants. Since it is impossible to know when you will reach saturation, it is difficult to specify a specific number of participants at the outset of the study. Therefore, it is better to identify the anticipated number of participants as a range in your initial study design and for your proposal rather than an exact number.

Data Sources (Interviews, Focus Groups, Observations) and Protocols

The most common source of data for qualitative studies is participant interviews. It is through in-depth interviews that we are able to learn about participants' experiences, thoughts, and perspectives and hear their personal stories related to the phenomenon under study. Many practical decisions must be made regarding interviews, including the structure of the interview, the questions to be asked, the location of the interview, how the interview will be captured (i.e., audio- or video-recorded), the length of the interview, and the number of times participants will be interviewed. A further consideration is the format of the interview, which will either be conducted with an individual or a group of individuals, typically called a focus group interview.

A primary consideration is the structure of the interview, which can vary from highly structured, with a predetermined set and order of questions, to unstructured, which is more open-ended and conversational. A semi-structured interview is a combination of the two and allows for flexibility in the interview process. Related to the structure of the interview are the questions to be asked during the interview, which is referred to as the interview protocol or interview guide. It is important to note that your interview protocol questions are different than your research questions.

Another consideration is the location of the interview. For example, will it take place in person in a private room at a public or university library, at the participants' home or place of employment, or in your office, or will it take place virtually via a videoconferencing platform or via social media? You must also plan for how the interview will be recorded (i.e., audio- or video-recorded) for later transcription.

The length of the interview is important to consider, as is the number of times participants will be interviewed. Finally, you must decide the format of the interviews and if participants will be interviewed individually or in a group, which is often referred to as a focus group interview. Rubin and Rubin (2012) provide extensive guidance for designing and conducting qualitative interviews in their text, *Qualitative Interviewing: The Art of Hearing Data* (2nd ed.).

Another common source of data for qualitative studies is an observation. As with interviews, decisions need to be made regarding where the observation will take place, how long the observation will last, and how information from the observation will be recorded. Merriam (2016) offers direction for planning and recording observations, as well as for determining the role of the researcher during the observations (e.g., complete participant, complete observer, etc.). Billups (2021) provides observational tools and templates that may be helpful for students. Many additional sources of data may be utilized in qualitative studies and can include such things as documents, artifacts, social media posts, art, and photos, as well as other physical matter. When deciding which sources of data may be included in the study, consider which sources are meaningful and beneficial for answering the research question.

Role of the Researcher

In qualitative research, the researcher is the primary instrument of data collection and analysis; this means that the relationship between the researcher and participants is an intimate one. Because of the researcher's close and personal relationship to participants, measures for ensuring trustworthiness or validity must be put into place to ensure that the researcher's biases and previous experiences with the topic do not interfere with data analysis. Measures of trustworthiness are discussed in more depth later in the chapter. As the primary instrument of data collection and analysis, the researcher can expect to spend extensive time in the field collecting data (e.g., interviewing, observing, gathering artifacts, etc.), as well as a great amount of time analyzing the data.

Methods of Data Analysis

Qualitative data analysis is "process of bringing order, structure, and meaning to the mass of data collected" (Bloomberg & Volpe, 2019, p. 231) and is considered "recursive and dynamic" (Merriam & Tisdell, 2016, p. 195). It is an inductive and complex process of making meaning of the data. According to Merriam and Tisdell (2016), data analysis "involves consolidating, reducing, and interpreting what people have said and what the researcher has seen and read" (p. 202). In short, data collected through interviews, observations, or other forms (e.g., documents, social media posts, artifacts, poems, etc.) are analyzed to answer your research question. Typically, data collection and data analysis occur simultaneously in qualitative research. Although the recommended methods of analysis vary for each of the qualitative approaches, in general qualitative data analysis involves the following:

- An interview is transcribed.
- The researcher reads the transcript and notes any bits of data (words, phrases, etc.) that are striking and relevant to the research question. This process is typically referred to as **coding**.
- Once codes are created, they are grouped or clustered into categories or themes.
- Each transcript is analyzed individually and then analyzed across cases, whereby patterns in the categories or themes are identified across transcripts.

Specific guidance regarding data analysis procedures for each qualitative approach is provided in the literature and should be followed accordingly to ensure methodological congruence and safeguard the trustworthiness of your findings. For example, if you are conducting a constructivist grounded theory study, you want to follow the data analysis methods recommended by Charmaz. It is important to reiterate that data collection and analysis typically occur simultaneously due to the emergent nature of qualitative research; it is generally impossible to know ahead of time every participant who may be interviewed, every question that may be asked, or how to proceed next until data are analyzed (Merriam & Tisdell, 2016).

Measures for Ensuring Trustworthiness (Validity)

Evaluation of qualitative research is critically important to ensure that the findings are valid. As with other concepts in qualitative research, different terminology is used by various authors in the field. In general, validation strategies are similar across all qualitative research; however, some validation measures may be specific to a given approach, such as the validation strategies of Yardley (2000) recommended for IPA. We have chosen to discuss Lincoln and Guba's (1985) measures for ensuring trustworthiness and Creswell and Poth's (2018) validation strategies.

Lincoln and Guba

Lincoln and Guba (1985) prefer terms that lean more toward naturalistic approaches as opposed to positivistic or quantitative methodologies. Measures for ensuring trustworthiness include ways to ensure credibility (internal validity), transferability (external validity), dependability (reliability), and confirmability (objectivity). The techniques these researchers recommend include prolonged engagement; persistent observation; triangulation (of sources, methods, investigators); peer debriefing; negative case analysis; referential inadequacy; member checks; thick descriptions; the dependability audit (including the **audit trail**); the confirmability audit (including the audit trail); and the researcher's reflexive journal. Each of the techniques will ensure certain aspects of trustworthiness of the study (e.g., thick descriptions ensure transferability), while some ensure trustworthiness for all areas (e.g., the researcher's reflexive journal ensures all areas of trustworthiness).

Creswell

Creswell (2016) presents validation strategies that are organized by various perspectives: the researcher's lens, the participant's lens, and the reader's lens. Strategies for validation from the researcher's perspective include corroborating evidence through triangulation (of multiple data sources, methods, or investigators), discovering negative case analysis or disconfirming evidence, and clarifying researcher bias by engaging in **reflexivity** for the duration of the study. From the participant's lens, he recommends seeking feedback from participants through member checking, ensuring prolonged engagement with participants and persistent observation in the field, and collaborating with participants throughout the study. Finally, from the reader's perspective, this researcher recommends enabling external audits from a consultant or auditor, generating rich and thick descriptions of participants and the setting, and participating in a peer review or debriefing of the data and research process. Researchers should engage in at least two of the validation strategies, with some being more cost-effective and easier to implement than others (Creswell, 2016).

Ethical Considerations

Every study involving humans must adhere to the standards established for protecting human subjects, and it is important to consider and plan for ethical issues that may arise at various points in the research process. Prior to beginning a study, IRB approval must be acquired from your university's IRB. Depending on the nature of the study, additional IRB approval may be necessary from the site (e.g., prison or hospital). Participant solicitation cannot begin until IRB approval is gained. During recruitment, potential participants should be made aware of the purpose of the study, and each will sign a form consenting to the study before data collection begins. Participants' identity should be protected during all stages of the research process. In addition to the use of pseudonyms, other measures may need to be taken to ensure that participants' identities are kept confidential.

All data (e.g., transcripts, photos, etc.) should be stored using adequate security measures, such as an encrypted thumb drive or password-protected computer. A further ethical consideration for qualitative research specifically is the relationship between researcher and participant. It is important to ensure boundaries are maintained throughout the research process; researcher reflexivity can provide a safeguard for relationship boundary issues (Billups, 2021).

Limitations and Delimitations of the Study

It is important to identify the limitations and delimitations of the study. The **limitations** of the study are outside of the control of the researcher. According to Bloomberg and Volpe (2019), "These are the constraints regarding transferability, applications to practice, and/or utility of findings that are the result of the ways in which you chose to design the study" (p. 207). These arise from implicit characteristics of the research design. For example, one limitation may be participant bias; the participants may have chosen to participate in the study because they feel strongly about the topic being studied.

Delimitations, on the other hand, are the intentional choices made by the researcher and indicate how they have chosen to narrow the scope of their study. In other words, not only does a researcher let the reader know what they chose to include (i.e., participants, time period, data collection and analysis methods, etc.), but also what they chose not to include (Bloomberg & Volpe, 2019). For example, you may have delimited participation in your study to master's students and did not included doctoral students because of the difference in their developmental levels.

Summary

Qualitative methodology is essential for answering certain research questions. Designing and conducting a qualitative study for one's dissertation research does not have to be an overwhelming process if you are adequately prepared to do so. Although qualitative research involves a large investment of time, the research process can be highly rewarding for the researcher while contributing in an important way to one's field.

Qualitative Research Resources

To assist in your qualitative research, the following resources have been provided. While not an exhaustive list, they provide good insights into the different types of research. Explore these and other options to help design your study along with consultation with your Chair and methodologist.

Case Study Research

Merriam, S. B., & Tisdell, E. J. (2016). *Qualitative research: A guide to design and implementation.* Jossey-Bass.
Stake, R. E. (1995). *The art of case study research.* SAGE.
Yazan, B. (2015). Three approaches to case study methods in education: Yin, Merriam, and Stake. *The Qualitative Report, 20*(2), 134–152.
Yin, R. K. (2018). *Case study research and applications: Design and Methods* (6th ed.). SAGE.

Conceptual Frameworks

Green, H. E. (2014). Use of theoretical and conceptual frameworks in qualitative research. *Nurse Researcher, 21*(6), 34–38. https://doi.org/10.7748/nr.21.6.34.e1252

Kivunja, C. (2018). Distinguishing between theory, theoretical framework, and conceptual framework: A systematic review of lessons from the field. *International Journal of Higher Education, 7*(6), 44. https://doi.org/10.5430/ijhe.v7n6p44

Ravitch, S. M., & Riggan, M. (2017). *Reason & rigor: How conceptual frameworks guide research* (2nd ed.). SAGE.

Data Analysis

Miles, M. B., Huberman, A. M., & Saldana, J. (2014). *Qualitative data analysis: A methods sourcebook* (3rd ed.). SAGE.

Saldana, J. (2016). *The coding manual for qualitative researchers* (3rd ed.). SAGE.

Data Collection

Billups, F. D. (2021). *Qualitative data collection tools: Design, development, and applications.* SAGE.

Rubin, H. J., & Rubin, I. S. (2012). *Qualitative interviewing: The art of hearing data* (3rd ed.). SAGE.

Ethnography

Fetterman, D. M. (2010). *Ethnography: Step-by-step* (3rd ed.). SAGE.

Wolcott, H. F. (2008). *Ethnography: A way of seeing* (2nd ed.). AltaMira.

Grounded Theory

Charmaz, K. (2014). *Constructing grounded theory* (2nd ed.). SAGE.

Corbin, J., & Strauss, A. (2015). *Basics of qualitative research: Techniques and procedures for developing grounded theory* (4th ed.). SAGE.

Interpretative Phenomenological Analysis

Smith, J. A., Flowers, P., & Larkin, M. (2009). *Interpretative phenomenological analysis: Theory, methods, and research.* SAGE.

Narrative

Clandinin, D. J. (Ed.) (2007). *Handbook of narrative inquiry: Mapping a methodology.* SAGE.

Clandinin, D. J. (2013). *Engaging in narrative inquiry.* Left Coast Press.

Riessman, C. K. (2008). *Narrative methods for the human sciences.* SAGE.

Phenomenology

Moustakas, C. (1994). *Phenomenological research methods.* SAGE.

Van Manen, M. (2014). *Phenomenology of practice: Meaning-giving methods in phenomenological research and writing.* Left Coast Press.

Qualitative Dissertations

Bloomberg, L. D., & Volpe, M. (2019). *Completing your qualitative dissertation: A roadmap from beginning to end* (4th ed.). SAGE.

Durdella, N. (2019). *Qualitative dissertation methodology: A guide for research design and methods.* SAGE.

Qualitative Research Methodology

Creswell, J. W., & Poth, C. N. (2018). *Qualitative inquiry & research design: Choosing among five approaches* (4th ed.). SAGE.

Denzin, N. K., & Lincoln, Y. S. (Eds.). (2018). *The SAGE handbook of qualitative research* (5th ed.). SAGE.

Maxwell, J. A. (2005). *Qualitative research design: An interactive approach* (2nd ed.). SAGE.

McCaslin, M. L., & Scott, K. W. (2003). The five-question method for framing a qualitative research study. *The Qualitative Report*, 8(3), 447–461.

Merriam, S. B., & Tisdell, E. J. (2016). *Qualitative research: A guide to design and implementation* (4th ed.). Jossey-Bass.

Lincoln, Y. S., & Guba, E. G. (1985). *Naturalistic inquiry*. SAGE.

References

Billups, F. D. (2021). *Qualitative data collection tools: Design, development, and applications*. SAGE.

Bloomberg, L. D., & Volpe, M. (2019). *Completing your qualitative dissertation: A roadmap from beginning to end* (4th ed.). SAGE.

Braun, V., & Clarke, V. (2013). *Successful qualitative research: A practical guide for beginners*. SAGE.

Creswell, J. W., & Poth, C. N. (2018). *Qualitative inquiry & research design: Choosing among five approaches* (4th ed.). SAGE.

Gelinas, L., Pierce, R., Winkler, S., Cohen, I. G., Lynch, H. F., & Bierer, B. E. (2017). Using social media as a research recruitment tool: Ethical issues and recommendations. *The American Journal of Bioethics*, 17(3), 3–14. https://doi.org/10.1080/15265161.2016.1276644

Kivunja, C. (2018). Distinguishing between theory, theoretical framework, and conceptual framework: A systematic review of lessons from the field. *International Journal of Higher Education*, 7(6), 44. https://doi.org/10.5430/ijhe.v7n6p44

Lincoln, Y. S., & Guba, E. G. (1985). *Naturalistic inquiry*. SAGE.

Lopez, K. A., & Willis, D. G. (2004). Descriptive versus interpretive phenomenology: Their contributions to nursing knowledge. *Qualitative Health Research*, 14(5), 726–735.

Maxwell, J. A. (2005). *Qualitative research design: An interactive approach* (2nd ed.). SAGE.

McCaslin, M. L., & Scott, K. W. (2003). The five-question method for framing a qualitative research study. *The Qualitative Report*, 8(3), 447–461.

Merriam, S. B. (1998). *Qualitative research and case study applications in education*. Jossey-Bass.

Merriam, S. B., & Tisdell, E. J. (2016). *Qualitative research: A guide to design and implementation* (4th ed.). Jossey-Bass.

Miles, M. B., Huberman, A. M., & Saldana, J. (2014). *Qualitative data analysis: A methods sourcebook* (3rd ed.). SAGE.

Ravitch, S. M., & Riggan, M. (2017). *Reason & rigor: How conceptual frameworks guide research* (2nd ed.). SAGE.

Riessman, C. K. (2008). *Narrative methods for the human sciences*. SAGE.

Rubin, H. J., & Rubin, I. S. (2012). *Qualitative interviewing: The art of hearing data* (3rd ed.). SAGE.

Sheperis, C. J., Young, J. S., & Daniels, M. H. (2017). *Counseling research: Quantitative, qualitative, and mixed methods*. Pearson.

Smith, J. A. (2004). Reflecting on the development of interpretative phenomenological analysis and its contribution to qualitative research in psychology. *Qualitative Research in Psychology*, 1, 39–45.

Smith, J. A. (2011). Evaluating the contribution of interpretative phenomenological analysis. *Health Psychology Review*, 5(1), 9–27.

Smith, J. A., Flowers, P., & Larkin, M. (2009). *Interpretative phenomenological analysis: Theory, methods, and research*. SAGE.

Stake, R. E. (1995). *The art of case study research*. SAGE.

Strauss, A., & Corbin, J. (1998). *Basics of qualitative research: Techniques and procedures for developing grounded theory* (2nd ed.). SAGE.

Wolcott, H. F. (2008). *Ethnography: A way of seeing* (2nd ed.). AltaMira.

Yardley, L. (2000). Dilemmas in qualitative health research. *Psychology & Health*, 15, 215–228.

Yazan, B. (2015). Three approaches to case study methods in education: Yin, Merriam, and Stake. *The Qualitative Report*, 20(2), 134–152.

Yin, R. K. (2002). *Case study research: Design and methods*. SAGE.

Worksheet 5.1: Qualitative Research Planner

Use the following steps to design your qualitative study. Remember, qualitative research is emergent and evolving. Study design is an iterative process, not a linear one. You may complete these steps out of order (depending on where you are in your process), and you may also return to each step numerous times for revisions as your study design emerges.

1. **Identify a research problem.**

   - What idea would you like to study? What is the key phenomenon (one key concept to be explored in two or three words only)?

     "The topic for the study will be …"

     _____

   - Why is this study important? What are the practical issues that lead to a need for the study? Provide a compelling argument for why the topic needs to be studied. Include deficiencies or gaps in the literature.

     "This study needs to be conducted because …"

     _____

     _____

     _____

     _____

2. **Begin designing your conceptual framework.**

   - Identify the key concepts, variables, constructs, and theories relevant to the topic being studied and the presumed interrelationships among them. It is recommended that you create a graphic representation and a narrative. Be prepared for many iterations of your conceptual framework.

3. **Identify the qualitative approach to be used.**

   - Identify which qualitative approach you will use for your study. The five-question method by McCaslin and Scott (2003) may help you decide which qualitative approach or genre is most appropriate for you study.

     _____

4. **Write a purpose statement.**

   - Use the purpose statement script provided by Creswell and Poth (2018) to write your purpose statement. If you are unsure of some aspects of your study, leave them blank and return to them later.

- Use the following for guidance on encoding words specific to your chosen approach:

  "The purpose of this _____ (narrative, phenomenological, grounded theory, ethnographic, case) study is to (was? will be?) to _____ (understand? describe? develop? discover?) the _____ (central phenomenon of the study) for _____ (participants) at _____ (the site). At this stage in the research, the _____ (central phenomenon) will be generally defined as _____ (a general definition of the central phenomenon)." (p. 132)

5. Write your central research question and sub-questions.

Central question

- Use this script to write your "grand-tour," open-ended primary research question.

  "_____ (how or what) do _____ (participants) at _____ (site) _____ (discover, explore, identify, describe) _____ (the central phenomenon)?"

Sub-questions

- Write sub-questions by breaking down the central question into smaller, more specific parts.

    a. _____

    b. _____

    c. _____

6. Collect data.

- Describe your methods for data collection. Include all of the following:

  Participants

  Describe the participants from whom you will collect data. The site may be included here (e.g., graduate counseling students at X university).

  _____

  _____

  Sampling strategy

  Identify the qualitative sampling strategy or strategies you will use to use to select your participants (e.g., criterion sampling, snowball sampling, convenience sampling, etc.).

  _____

  _____

  _____

Recruitment procedures

Identify how you will solicit or recruit participants (e.g., email, flyer, electronic mailing list announcement, etc.).

_____

_____

Data sources

List the sources of data you will collect (e.g., interviews, observations, documents, artifacts, etc.).

_____

_____

_____

Data collection protocols

Describe the data collection protocols to be utilized (e.g., semi-structured interview, observation protocol, etc.).

_____

_____

_____

Interview protocol questions

Create the questions you will ask participants in order to answer your research question(s). (Note that these are *not* your research questions.)

a. _____

b. _____

c. _____

d. _____

e. _____

7. **Analyze the data.**

    Describe the methods, steps, or procedures you will use to analyze your data. These are typically specific to your chosen approach or genre.

_____

8. **Determine the validity/measures for ensuring trustworthiness.**

   Describe how you will establish the credibility of your study (e.g., triangulation, peer review/debriefing, member checking, audit trail, reflexivity, etc.).

   _____
   _____
   _____

9. **Consider ethics.**

   Describe how you will attend to all ethical issues throughout the study (e.g., IRB approval, use pseudonyms for confidentiality of participants, etc.).

   _____
   _____
   _____

CHAPTER 6

Quantitative Methodology

By Michell L. Temple, PhD, EdD, CRC, NCC

The decision to utilize a quantitative research tradition for a doctoral dissertation begins with your rationale. You must first decide the significance of precision through statistical analysis to answer the research questions that are the focus of the study. Since quantitative research allows researchers to investigate behaviors, beliefs, and attitudes precisely and narrowly within a specific population, choosing a quantitative design often suggests that the constructs are measurable and observable. With this in mind, you may reflect on this question: *Why is it important to examine the constructs of interests numerically?* Once you have answered that question, you will need to gather information from a thorough literature review to inform the design and implementation of your quantitative study. Conducting quantitative research can be a time-consuming and frustrating experience, a timely and enjoyable one, or anything in between. A quantitative study offers you a chance to master specific statistical analyses and an opportunity to contribute to your field. The quantitative research chapter that follows intends to assist you with crafting and completing a methodological rigorous quantitative study.

Overview of Quantitative Methodology

Quantitative research philosophically presumes that knowledge is discoverable through objective observations measuring the natural variations in existing situations (McBurney & White, 2004; McGregor, 2018). It is conducted when researchers want to derive knowledge from experiments, the manipulation of variables, or by assessing existing knowledge with numerical precision (McGregor, 2018). **Quantitative research** involves describing, predicting, controlling, or explaining causal connections or noncausal associations through the application of scientific methods (Creswell, 2014; McGregor, 2018). Scientific methods include standardized assumptions and rules and procedures for collecting and analyzing data, strategies to reduce inherent researcher bias, and processes for generating credible knowledge (Heppner et al., 2016). In sum, quantitative methodology requires phenomena of interest to be researchable numerically in a systematic and logical manner.

Like the foundational concepts of ontology, epistemology, axiology, and methodology used to frame qualitative research in Chapter 5 of this book, it is also crucial to comprehend these philosophical underpinnings within quantitative research. McBurney and White (2004) and Heppner et al. (2016) explicate these shared positivistic and postpositivistic assumptions of quantitative researchers: The factual nature of realism can only be discovered by evaluating the falsifiability of theories; knowledge awaits discovery via the application of scientific methods; it attempts to articulate causality, laws of behaviors, and principles that provide explanations leading to predictions and control of phenomena. It is important to note there are differences in the positivistic and postpositivistic assumptions that influence quantitative researchers' beliefs about truth and the role of the researcher.

Heppner et al. (2016) provide helpful insights into assumptive differences between positivistic and postpositivistic paradigms that inform the application of quantitative methods in social science inquiry. First, the views differ in that postpositivism purports that truth cannot be fully known, only approximated through a body of corroborating research, while positivism asserts truth can be known via the application of scientific experimental designs. Second, the researcher within the postpositivistic framework has biases that affect the research, denouncing the possibility of an objective researcher ascribed to the positivistic approach.

Scholars conclude that quantitative research within the social sciences incorporates positivistic and postpositivistic tenets. Creswell (2014), Heppner et al. (2016), and McBurney and White (2004) provide these essential elements of quantitative research:

- Designs include experimental, quasi-experimental, or nonexperimental scientific methods of inquiry
- Operationalizes constructs or phenomena of interest with objective instruments
- Attempts to control factors that may contaminate the study of the phenomena
- Strives for generalizability to a specific population based on the findings from a sample population
- Researcher follows a linear plan to conduct the study with little or no deviation
- Applies standards of validity and reliability
- Involves statistical analysis to make meaning of data collected from instruments
- Applies deductive reasoning to formulate probabilistic truth statements

The list of quantitative research elements can be used to guide the development of a methodologically appropriate study. Designing a solid quantitative study for your dissertation will take time and effort; however, the time well spent will provide you with a solid foundation to implement and finish doctoral-level research.

Goals and Purpose

In the overview, you were advised to answer this question to consider quantitative methodology and methods as viable options for your dissertation research: *Why is it important to numerically examine the constructs of interests?* The question was posed to you early because a well-planned quantitative research study connects the research problem to the purpose statement and research questions. Knowing the rationale for a precise measurement of the observations can prepare you to align your study with the goals and purpose of quantitative research. Remember, quantitative researchers design studies that describe, predict, control, or explain causal or noncausal associations using scales of measurement, also known as instrumentation (Creswell, 2014; McGregor, 2018). Quantitative research goals and purposes depend on applying scientific methods to confirm or explore objective observations. Specifically, McGregor (2018) indicates,

> The scientific method includes confirmatory and explanatory science. The confirmatory scientific method involves posing and testing hypotheses and models that allow people to describe, explain, and modify the real world. The explanatory scientific method involves making observations, searching for patterns and then making tentative conclusions or generalizations about how some aspect of the world operates. (pp. 255–256)

Often quantitative researchers conduct studies to generate new knowledge, investigate the falsifiability of current knowledge, or examine the relationships among theories through hypothesis testing (Heppner et al., 2016). These reasons for conducting quantitative research represent some common applications of confirmatory and explanatory scientific methods. If you have determined that objective observations and numerical precision are important to your dissertation study, then quantitative research is an excellent choice.

Role of Theory and Type of Variables in Quantitative Research

Before we discuss the types of quantitative research, we will review the role of theory and the types of variables in quantitative research inquiry. These two factors will inform your choice of quantitative research design. Theory and variables in quantitative research complement each other. Theory refers to an interrelated set of constructs, meaning an attribute or characteristic, formed into propositions, or hypotheses, which specify the relationship between variables and the observable and measurable presentation of a construct (Creswell, 2014; McBurney & White, 2004). Theory establishes the theoretical rationale among variables. McGregor (2018) identifies exploratory, descriptive, relational, and explanatory as types of theory utilized in research inquiry. **Exploratory theory** tests or pilots a new method or instrument, whereas **descriptive theory** articulates the characteristics of the phenomena and the key variables that influence it. **Relational theory** identifies and explains relationships between variables. **Explanatory theory** finds and accounts for causal relationships. Theory in quantitative research positions a study within the applicable scientific method (ontological and methodological paradigms), confirmatory or explanatory, and a testable theoretical rationale (epistemological and axiological paradigms).

The understanding of theory also informs the selection and relationship of variables within quantitative research. Creswell (2014) and McBurney and White (2004) define a variable as a construct of a person, place, or thing that can be measured or observed within a given situation and produce scores that vary into at least two exclusive groups. Variables are classified by temporal order and scales of measurement (Creswell, 2014; McBurney & White, 2004).

Creswell (2014) explains that **temporal order** refers to the presented sequence of variables that reflect the probability of effect of one variable on another, which informs the formulation of predictions. **Independent variables** represent characteristics that affect outcomes or

dependent variables, which connote the measurable outcomes. **Intervening or mediating variables** are attributes in the middle of independent and dependent variables that could influence the dependent variable. **Moderating variables** are other independent variables that affect either the direction or strength of the relationship between the independent and dependent variables of interest. **Control (covariate)** variables are a unique type of independent variable that can potentially influence the dependent variable; however, **confounding variables** often exist outside of the parameters of the study but might influence the variables of interest indirectly. Researchers account for the temporal order of variables in research questions and hypotheses.

McBurney and White (2004) and Tabachnick and Fidell (2019) categorize variables by type and scales of measurement, also called instrumentation. Each type and scale correspond with a quantitative method and analytical approach. Categorical, discrete, and continuous are the three types of quantitative variables that can be created from scales of measurement. **Categorical variables** vary in nature, such as people, places, or things. **Nominal scales** of measurement classify objects or events into categorical variables by assigning numbers to represent variations within observations (McBurney & White, 2004). **Discrete variables** represent categories too, but as finite and small values that are organized by rank or the representation of the value of distinct occurrences (Tabachnick & Fidell, 2019). **Ordinal scales of measurement** organize objects or events in order of importance or magnitude along a continuum, but nominal scales can also be used to categorize the variations (McBurney & White, 2004; Tabachnick & Fidell, 2019). Both nominal and ordinal scales of measurement lack a smooth progression from a category or one numerical value. Tabachnick and Fidell (2019) highlight that the differences between discrete and continuous variables are not always clear because of ordinal scales. Researchers emphasize that **continuous variables** are distinguishable from discrete variables when values fall along a continuum and are not limited to specific values (McBurney & White, 2004; Tabachnick & Fidell, 2019). **Interval and ratio scales** measure values continuously and not in steps. Categorizing variables by type and scales of measurements aids quantitative researchers in the development of research questions and the selection of instrumentation. A researcher who conducts a thorough literature review has a foundation to craft a solid quantitative research study that has both a clear theoretical framework and the capability of investigating, and measuring identified variables accordingly.

Types of Quantitative Research and Considerations of Each

Once a researcher decides to conduct a quantitative study, they are tasked with choosing an appropriate research design to investigate and measure the identified variables while "ruling out as many plausible rival hypotheses or explanations as possible" (Heppner et al., 2016, p. 119). Therefore, it is important for researchers to carefully consider the strengths and weaknesses of the types of research designs based on the concepts of internal and external validity, which are associated with experimental control and generalizability (Heppner et al. 2016). **Internal validity** constitutes the extent to which a researcher can determine causal relationships due to the amount of control of these factors in the study: the selection process of the sample of participants from the target population, the assignment procedures of the sample to groups, and the degree of manipulation of study variables. **External validity** establishes the scope of applicability of the study results to the real world related to the study conditions such as population, treatment, outcomes, and settings (Heppner et al., 2016). You are encouraged to review a research methods textbook for detailed information about the distinct types and implications of threats to internal and external validity.

Research Design Rationale

Some researchers consider the research problem and questions, their personal experience, and the consumers of their study results when selecting the overall research approach (Creswell, 2014). Others may select a design per the four criteria outlined in Heppner et al. (2016): existing knowledge about the research question, inferences made to create the present knowledge base via research design, resources and costs associated with research designs, and threats to internal and external validity. Regardless of whose criteria a researcher follows, the empirical-analytic approach of quantitative research necessitates a strong rationale for a selected research design (McGregor, 2018).

Experimental Designs

Experimental designs, often referred to as *true* experimental designs, indicate that a researcher wants to investigate treatments or interventions through the application of scientific methods (e.g., testing a hypothesis; Houser, 2020). The key characteristics of experimental designs include a random selection of the sample of participants from the target population, random assignment of the sample to groups, the manipulation of an independent variable(s), and objective measurement of any changes in the dependent variable with the intent of drawing causal inferences (Heppner et al., 2016; Houser, 2020; McGregor, 2018). McGregor (2018) and Heppner et al. (2016) describe experimental designs based on participants and the timing of objective measurements. Research designs according to participants are known as between-subject designs or factorial designs (comparisons of two or more groups) and within-group designs (a single group). McGregor and Heppner et al. also discuss single-subject design (a single person) designs. Researchers interested in the latter design should review case study designs for guidance. Experimental designs by the timing of the administration of instrumentation are posttest only and pretest-posttest control group designs.

Between-subject, factorial, and comparative experimental designs incorporate a control or a comparison group. A **control group** refers to a group of study participants who do not receive treatment, whereas a **comparison group** means a group of study participants who receive an alternative treatment or intervention that the researcher compares to the treatment provided to the experimental group (Houser, 2020). **Between-group or between-subject** designs, sometimes called comparative designs, "compare between different treatment groups and/or with control groups" (Heppner et al., 2016, p. 245). **Factorial designs** may or may not use a control group but do simultaneously study two or more independent variables and their interactive effects on a dependent variable (Heppner et al., 2016). Another type of between-subject design is a **dependent samples experiment**, which assigns participants to groups randomly per an assumption about a variable that researchers want to account or control for in the study.

Houser (2020) notes that the groups of participants by intervention are commonly labeled as the independent variable(s) because the treatment is influencing them. Subsequently, the dependent variable typically refers to the variables measured throughout the study. In dependent samples designs, researchers may label the variable of interest as a control or confounding variable.

When planning their studies, researchers consider the strengths and weaknesses of between-subject, factorial, and comparative experimental designs. Heppner et al. (2016) state that the overall strength of between-group designs lies in the procedures that control for many threats to internal validity, such as controlling the amount of time that passes during the experiment and the potential for developmental changes in the participants. Yet the generalizability or external validity of between-group designs can be limited to the study population and no other groups, typically when the study sample is not representative of the target population. Between-group experimental designs often are less applicable in applied settings because of the organic nature of the environments.

An inherent strength of factorial designs is their ability to study two or more independent variables and their interactive effects on a dependent variable, which adds complexity to the general between-group design. The strength of the increased number of independent variables also poses a potential weakness of factorial designs. The additional complexity and analytical capability of factorial designs can decrease the power of a statistical analysis. Heppner et al. (2016) state that researchers should limit independent variables to those with theoretical and empirical applicability to the research questions.

In **within-subject experimental designs**, researchers expose participants to all treatment conditions, and participants serve as their control. Therefore, participants must be randomly assigned to different sequences of the intervention. There are two common types of within-subject experimental designs, crossover and counterbalance. A **crossover design** requires participants to switch from one experimental condition to another, representing two independent variables, at a specified time in the study (Heppner et al., 2016). During the course research, objective observations through instrumentation measure the changes in the various treatments. The **counterbalanced crossover design** attempts to control for the order of participant exposure to interventions (Heppner et al., 2016). The instrumentation researchers utilize in a counterbalanced crossover design includes a pretest, a measure when the groups change treatments, and a measurement at the end of treatment or posttest.

Heppner et al. (2016) outline five strengths and limitations of the utility of within-subject designs to answer certain research questions. As with between-subject designs, an inherent strength of within-subject experimental designs is in the prescribed procedures of assigning participants and the manipulation of independent variables, allowing researchers to control for threats of internal validity and strengthening external validity. Statistical power in the design comes from all participants being included in all treatments.

A limitation of within-subject experimental designs might be the amount of time necessary to conduct the study. Heppner et al. (2016) suggest that these designs take longer to conduct because of the time required to expose all participants to all treatments. These authors also note that order effects, as mentioned in the crossover and counterbalance crossover designs, threaten internal validity and are difficult to control. This design has limitations on the research questions it can answer, such that independent variables can only be manipulated unidirectionally and the variations of a single group restrict the complexity of within-group analysis.

Two typical between-group experimental designs are posttest only and pretest-posttest control group designs (Heppner et al., 2016), which also account for the timing of the objective observations in relation to the treatment or intervention. Timing specifies when study participants complete the instruments. **Posttest only control group designs** mean that the measure is administered after the treatment. **Pretest-posttest control group designs** indicate that variables are measured before and after the intervention.

Both posttest and pretest-posttest control group designs control for most of the threats to internal validity by allowing researchers to potentially evidence causal relationship differences between the experimental and control groups based on the changes measured by the dependent variable (Heppner et al., 2016). Scholars suggest that the posttest-only control group designs render pretest observations unnecessary to evidence causality with a statistically significant difference in groups (Heppner et al., 2016; Houser, 2020). However, Heppner et al. (2016) argue that posttest-only control group designs do not control for threats to external validity. Heppner et al. note that generalizability to other populations in posttest-only designs is questionable and prescribed by participants' responses to experimental conditions.

The pretest or pretreatment objective observation collected in a pretest-posttest control group design offers researchers statistical options unavailable in the posttest-only control group design (Heppner et al., 2016). Pretest measures allow researchers to reduce the effects of differences in participants as a covariate variable, describe study participants, and analyze the change in the dependent variable. Heppner et al. (2016) assert that the weaknesses in pretest-posttest control group designs lie mostly in how researchers utilize the pretest scores in statistical analysis. Researchers are discouraged from comparing the gain scores, the change in pretest and posttest scores, in analysis because there are multiple alternative explanations for differences. Sensitization to the posttest by the pretest is one of many threats to external validity when gain scores are used in pretest and posttest designs.

Quasi-Experimental Designs

Quasi-experimental designs are another type of quantitative research that provides researchers with similar benefits to *true experimental* designs while using study participants in existing groups or those not randomly assigned to groups (Houser, 2020; McGregor, 2018). The design is beneficial because it involves the manipulation of variables and a control group or comparison group (McGregor, 2018). Quasi-experimental designs can use the procedures of between-group, within-group, posttest-only, and pretest-posttest designs. Like experimental designs, quasi-experimental designs emphasize the selection of participants and the timing of objective observations; however, quasi-experimental designs require the researcher to describe the nature of the existing groups.

The selection of quasi-experimental design relies heavily on the researcher's rationale for studying existing groups. A main concern in using existing groups in the research is selection by threat, the interaction effect between treatment and groups that affect internal validity. Researchers are encouraged to carefully consider the reasons for including certain groups, such as the purpose of the study, research questions, the potential effects on the dependent variable(s), and the generalizability of results (Heppner et al., 2016).

Sometimes researchers may not have access to an appropriate control or comparison groups in quasi-experimental studies. These are called **nonequivalent groups designs** because group comparisons are made within and between preexisting groups (Heppner et al., 2016). We will briefly look at the interpretable nonequivalent groups, including time-series designs, as these quasi-experimental designs may be more applicable to crafting and implementing a solid quantitative research study.

Cohorts are common and naturally occurring nonequivalent groups. They represent existing and nonrandom groups within applied settings that have similar conditions. Researchers can strengthen quasi-experimental research with cohorts when applying the various designs outlined in this section. Specifically, "researchers can argue conceptually and empirically that the two cohorts did, in fact, share similar environments, except of course for the treatment" (Heppner et al., 2016, p. 277). Researchers who use cohorts as their participant selection process, unlike other nonequivalent groups, can consider posttest-only designs because study participants progress through an established system at different periods and can take the posttest at similar times. The researchers within the established system can experiment or introduce an intervention in one cohort, but not another, then administer the objective measures according to the selected design.

Pretest-posttest design requires the researcher to administer a pretest on the dependent variable to at least two groups of study participants, experimental and control or comparison (Heppner et al., 2016). Researchers then engage the experimental group in the treatment. At the end of treatment, the posttest is administered to both groups.

Similar to experimental pretest-posttest designs, there are challenges and strengths to quasi-experimental designs with nonequivalent groups. Researchers are cautioned to avoid overgeneralizing any equivalence or similarities found on the pretest dependent variables as those results represent only the singular dimension and not all preexisting characteristics of groups (Heppner et al., 2016). The continued presence of selection-by-threat interaction and the potential issues with external validity are discussed in experimental designs such as pretest sensitization (Heppner et al., 2016) The pretest on the dependent variable strengthens the interpretability of the nonequivalent groups design because it examines and accounts for some pretreatment differences. The pretest also gives researchers some confidence in the observed differences between groups based on the posttest observations (e.g., a difference attributed to experimental manipulation). Issues with the statistical application of pretest observations remain in quasi-experimental designs. Please review the previous section on pretest-posttest experimental designs for details.

The proxy pretest measure refers to sensitizing participants to the experimental intervention through administering a similar but different pretest dependent variable (Heppner et al., 2016). Researchers concerned about pretest sensitization or using archival data and traditional pretest procedures may consider the proxy pretest design. Research participants complete the proxy pretest, then after the experimental group receives the treatment, both groups complete the posttest, which must be theoretical and testable with the pretest. Researchers explain and justify said relationship through a review of the research literature. The relationship between the proxy pretest and posttest serves as the primary concern for the viability of this design. Careful consideration must be given to the plans to analyze and interpret the results from the objective measures.

Secondary pretest design utilizes the standard pretest-posttest procedures with an additional pretest measure to increase the interpretability of results (Heppner et al., 2016). The secondary pretest allows researchers to examine a **characterological variable** that could represent varying degrees of participant maturation. Researchers administer the pretest on the dependent variable and the secondary pretest on a selection characteristic within the study groups. After the intervention with the experimental group concludes, both groups take the posttest. The secondary pretest may be administered with the posttest or used as a covariate, as described in experimental designs.

Time-series designs allow researchers to obtain multiple objective observations over time (Heppner et al., 2016). Characteristically, the observations involve the same or similar participants over the course of the intervention. The period when intervention or treatment occurs represents the interruption because researchers compare the measurements pre- and postinterruption to investigate the variables of interest. The most common types of time-series design are simple-interrupted and interrupted time series with nonequivalent dependent variables (Heppner et al., 2016). Simple-interrupted time series measures the same number of pre- and postinterruptions of study participants, whereas interrupted time series with nonequivalent dependent variables measures two dependent variables pre- and postinterruption. Both approaches add complexity to statistical analysis and support the control of internal validity issues.

Nonexperimental (Descriptive) Designs

Nonexperimental or descriptive designs are the final type of quantitative research. These designs provide quantitative insight into the characteristics or effects of a specific group (Heppner et al., 2016). Typically, descriptive designs are applied in the early stages of scientific exploration of phenomena as they naturally occur within a group of people (Heppner et al., 2016). Researchers who use descriptive designs can exclude the participant selection procedures outlined in experimental or quasi-experimental designs. Researchers also do not need to manipulate the independent variable(s). However, researchers can apply nonexperimental designs using group and within-group designs like experimental designs. Researchers select a descriptive design to describe a phenomenon, test theoretical conjectures, describe relationships among variables, and explore the presence of possible causal relationships (Heppner et al., 2016).

Instrumentation is a key component of descriptive designs. Heppner et al. (2016) state firmly, "The utility of descriptive designs is directly dependent on the quality of the instruments or assessments used to describe the phenomena" (p. 286). In descriptive designs, researchers investigate the phenomena using objective or standardized measures of the phenomena of interest. Consequently, researchers need to understand what they want to observe, the construct or phenomena of interest, and *how* they will measure said observations (Heppner et al., 2016). Four types of descriptive designs identified by Houser (2020) include survey, observational, correlational, and causal comparative.

The first two types of descriptive research, survey and observational, relate to the person providing the answers or respondent. Survey designs use self-reports to describe, explain, or explore facts, opinions, behaviors, attitudes, perceptions, and beliefs, as well as the relationship among these factors within a target population (Heppner et al., 2016; Houser, 2020). The respondent in survey designs is often from the target population and possibly experiences the phenomena of interest. Observational descriptive designs attempt to describe behaviors of interest within a specific group through the objective observation of others or raters (Houser, 2020). The respondent in observational designs is not the person exhibiting the behavior, but someone who has or can respond to an objective measure about the manifestation of the behavior within the target population. This design attempts to mitigate the internal and external validity issues of measures based on self-report. Observational designs still must contend with validity issues related to the raters.

The last two types of descriptive research, correlational and causal comparative, describe the application of data collected using surveys and observational instruments. **Correlational descriptive designs** seek to identify and understand the associations among variables through inferential statistics (Houser, 2020; McGregor, 2018). These designs allow researchers to describe how one variable relates to another variable as the variables change, but it cannot determine causal relationships. Correlational designs are variable-centered correlational research designs since researchers can include multiple variables within research questions and use more statistically sophisticated methods to analyze the data. **Causal comparative designs** identify the effects of naturally occurring variables ex post facto, after the fact (Houser, 2020). Researchers can examine between-group differences after distinct experiences to explain or predict some variable of interest.

TABLE 6.1 Types of Quantitative Research With Designs

TYPE	EXPERIMENTAL	QUASI-EXPERIMENTAL	NONEXPERIMENTAL
Purpose	Investigate treatments or interventions through the application of scientific methods (e.g., random sampling methods and testing a hypothesis)	Investigate treatments or interventions while using study participants who are in existing groups or those who are not randomly assigned to groups	Describe characteristics or the effects of events for an identified population
Designs	Between-group or between-subject Within-subject Posttest-only control group Pretest-posttest control group Dependent samples	Nonequivalent groups Cohorts Between-group or between-subject Within-subject Posttest-only group Pretest-posttest Proxy pretest measure Secondary pretest Simple-interrupted time series Interrupted time series with nonequivalent dependent variable measures	Survey Observational descriptive Correlational descriptive Causal comparative

Discussion of Methodology: Designing a Quantitative Study

Now that we have thoroughly discussed quantitative research methodology and types, let us now turn our attention to designing a quantitative study for your dissertation research. The quantitative research design process described in most research textbooks direct readers to apply the scientific method to ensure methodological congruence. Steps in the scientific method include identifying the problem through a thorough literature review; developing the purpose of the study, research questions, and hypotheses; describing sampling, instrumentation, and data collection procedures; and explaining plans for data analysis.

Research Problem

Ideally, you have chosen a research topic for your dissertation because the research problem or direction of inquiry stems from the overall focus of the study. The research problem represents the identified issue a study intends to address (McGregor, 2018). The literature review documents a researchable problem by illustrating gaps in the previous inquiry and defining the addressable issue within the research topic (Houser, 2020).

Quantitative research problems are often articulated as relational, difference, and descriptive problems (McGregor, 2018). Relational problems examine the association between variables. Difference problems investigate the dissimilarities among two or more phenomena of interest. Descriptive problems illuminate naturally occurring phenomena within a specific population that would benefit from further study because of limited knowledge, theory, or research. Framing a quantitative research problem as relational, difference, or descriptive within the literature review situates a research study to apply scientific methods.

Purpose of the Study

A research purpose statement declaratively expresses the specific issue the study will address (McGregor, 2018). It reflects a benchmark of methodological congruence in research studies. The statement typically uses this sentence stem: "The purpose of this study," which makes it easily locatable and recognizable to readers.

For quantitative studies, characteristics of a quality research purpose statement include an appropriate stem using keywords such as "purpose," "intent," or "objective"; if applicable, the theory, model, or conceptual framework; type of quantitative study and design; list of all variables of interest in order; incorporation of relational (relationship), difference (comparison), and descriptive (describe) research language; and the target population. Creswell (2014) provides this quantitative purpose statement script based on characteristics of a quality research statement:

> The purpose of this _____ (experimental, quasi-experimental, descriptive/nonexperimental) study is (was? will be?) to test the theory of _____ that _____ (describes outcomes) or (compares? relates?) the _____ (independent variable) to _____ (dependent variable), controlling for _____ (control variables) for _____ (participants) at _____ (the research site). (p. 130)

Another example of a purpose statement that includes the general elements follows:

> The purpose of this quantitative study (is, will be, or was) to _____ (examine, investigate, test, assess, evaluate, describe) the _____ (influence, characteristics, relationship) of _____ (state the phenomena or phenomenon of interest) in _____ (state the target population with a specific location or setting).

Both types of purpose statements are acceptable because they incorporate the standard elements of a quality statement. Regardless of which statement you choose for your dissertation, you need to identify and define independent and dependent variables. Creswell (2014) recommends defining key variables in the purpose statement; however, in the second purpose statement example, researchers define key variables in the "Definition of Terms" section of a dissertation.

Research Questions and Hypotheses

Research questions and hypotheses usually follow the purpose statement in a dissertation. Research questions interrogatively articulate the inquiry of the study, whereas hypotheses reflect the researcher's informed prediction of the answer to research questions (McGregor, 2018). The formation of research questions relates to the research problem and purpose statement. Research questions form interrogative sentences that can begin with words like "what," "to what extent," "is," and "does" (Creswell, 2014). They also utilize similar words found in purpose statements such as "relationship," "difference," "compare," "predict," "change over time," and "describe" (Houser, 2020). Since quantitative research utilizes instruments to measure the phenomena of interest, research questions should incorporate the following: _____ (phenomena of interest) as measured by scores from _____ (instrument).

Hypothesis testing is a central feature of scientific methods. To test a hypothesis, researchers must utilize statistical procedures to make inferences about the target population based on the study sample (Creswell, 2014). Most quantitative research dissertations will state a null (no difference) and alternative (prediction of difference) hypothesis for each research question.

Participants and Sample Size Justification

As you plan your study, you must decide the methods you will use to identify and access a sample population from the target population. Thus, researchers must describe the demographics of the study participants, which are the characteristics within the target population, and the overall group of interest, which will be included and excluded from the study (Houser, 2020). Those individuals who have the characteristics of interest from the target populations establish a sample population, a fraction of the group of interest (Heppner et al., 2016).

Since quantitative studies employ inferential statistics, scholars recommend that researchers determine the sample size and number of study participants necessary to conduct their selected analysis with statistical power and decrease the likelihood of type I and type II errors (Heppner et al., 2016; Huck, 2008; Tabachnick & Fidell, 2019). A priori statistical power analysis allows researchers to predetermine the probability that the selected statistical analysis will result in a rejection of the null hypothesis based on sample size, level of significance, the direction of hypothesis testing, and effect size (Houser, 2020). Software programs such as G*Power and IBM SPSS Sample Power3 offer this feature. The number of participants varies by experimental and nonexperimental survey designs. A minimum of 15 people per group in experimental designs and 100 participants for nonexperimental or descriptive designs is often recommended (Houser, 2020).

Describing participants of the study includes sampling methods, which refer to the procedures to identify and secure people to participate in a research study (Houser, 2020). Sampling methods in quantitative research influence the precision of the accuracy of scientific methods due to hypothesis testing and applicability to the target population (Huck, 2008). Specifically, when researchers use **probability sampling procedures**, meaning all members of the target population have an equally random chance to participate in the study, the educated guesses and generalizability from the sample to the target population are more statistically precise because these procedures align best with the mathematical underpinnings of inferential statistics (Huck, 2008). Researchers can also employ **nonprobability sampling methods**, denoting participants of the study are drawn from a readily accessible population and based on a specific study criterion, which decreases the statistical accuracy of hypothesis testing and limits generalizability to the target population (Huck, 2008). **Response rates**, the percentage of a target population who respond to a survey, also limit the generalizability of study results. The most well-known sampling methods for probability sampling and nonprobability sampling are in Table 6.2.

TABLE 6.2 Sampling Methods as Described by Houser (2020) and McBurney and White (2004)

TYPE OF SAMPLING	SAMPLING PROCEDURES	
Probability sampling methods	Simple random	Every member in a population has an equal chance of being chosen
	Stratified random	A set of individuals from the population who represent subgroups
	Systematic random	A limited number of individuals from the population selected based on a numerical pattern
	Cluster	Random sample of intact groups
Nonprobability sampling methods	Purposive	Nonrandom sample of people who are chosen for specific characteristics they posses
	Convenience	Nonrandom sample of a population that is available and readily accessible

Instrumentation and Considerations

Choosing instruments to include in your study involves exploring multiple facets of each item. The types of instruments available vary according to what they are assessing, and the criteria for selecting each will depend on your study's design, population, and research questions. Any instrument used in your study will need to be described in detail to increase replicability.

Types of Instruments

Remember, instruments, or **instrumentation** in social science research, refer to the objective observations, that standardize the rules for measuring a phenomenon. The review of types of variables and scales earlier in this chapter described the types of variables, categorical or continuous, calculated by the types of scales of measurements. Take special note of the type of scale used in an instrument because the score the scale produces informs the statistical analysis selected to answer the research question.

Three types of instruments include intact, modified, and researcher-developed instruments (Creswell, 2014). **Intact instruments** are preexisting self-report inventories, rating scales, or surveys that have been evaluated for validity and reliability. When choosing an intact instrument, researchers reference validation studies to support their rationale for selecting instruments because these studies provide helpful insight into the phenomena the instrument was designed to measure, validity, and how well the instrument measures the phenomena, reliability. Researchers also state that previous research did not include certain populations. If researchers choose to use an intact instrument within a new population, ethically, the study procedures should include instrument validation (Heppner et al., 2016).

Modified instruments are preexisting self-report inventories, rating scales, or surveys that were changed to measure another phenomenon of interest (Creswell, 2014). Researchers often modify a preexisting survey because the new phenomenon is similar to that of a preexisting survey (Heppner et al., 2016). Though intact instruments may have published validation studies, researchers cannot rely on previous research to report validity and reliability for use in their study due to the modifications to the survey. Consequently, researchers must validate the modified instrument and report the results (Creswell, 2014).

Researcher-developed instruments refer to self-report inventories, rating scales, or surveys designed by the researcher to use in the current study. The process of developing a new psychometrically sound instrument takes an intensive literature review, field or pilot testing, and statistical validation as part of the research process (Heppner et al., 2016). Most doctoral-level research utilizes intact and modified instruments unless scale construction is the focus of the dissertation study.

Criteria to Select an Intact Instrument

The process of selecting an intact instrument begins with reviewing validation studies. Researchers publish validation studies for intact instruments to describe the psychometric properties, types of validity, and reliability achieved by the instrument based on a population (Huck, 2008). **Validity** refers to the type of significant and valuable conclusions from the scores, and **reliability** means consistency and stability of scores over time (Creswell, 2014). Scholars disagree on specific factors to report validity and recommend that studies report at least two types of validity testing (Heppner et al., 2016). For evaluating reliability, it is recommended that researchers report two tests of reliability (Heppner et al., 2016; Houser, 2020). The preferred reliability estimate of internal consistency (Cronbach's Alpha) is .70 or higher (Heppner et al., 2016).

Describing Instruments

Once you have selected the instruments to measure the variables of interest, you need to provide a detailed overview of each measure. Creswell (2014) offers these elements as viable descriptors of an instrument in a research study:

- State the developer(s).
- Describe the process of obtaining permission to use or modify (e.g., actual permission from the developer or within the public domain).
- Outline the purpose of scales and subscales, design of items, including the type of scale of measurement.
- Provide sample questions.

- Detail the scoring procedures and interpretation of scores.
- Articulate the psychometric soundness by stating validity and reliability procedures and statistics based on study populations from previous research.

Data Collection Methods

Obtaining responses from the population of interest requires careful planning to ensure accuracy within the collected data. The data collection methods of quantitative research depend on the type and design of the research study. All ethically conducted research studies articulate procedures for recruitment and informed consent. However, experimental, quasi-experimental, and descriptive designs employ different procedures to collect data to control for threats of internal and external validity (Heppner et al., 2016). In experimental and quasi-experimental designs, data collection procedures include detailed explanations of the treatments and when and how participants will complete the selected instruments or measures (Heppner et al., 2016; McGregor, 2018). In descriptive designs, researchers describe the mechanisms and platforms they will use to distribute instruments for the target population to complete (Creswell, 2014). Mechanisms refer to the mode of distribution, email, electronic mailing lists, and social media, while platforms mean web-based surveys and rating scales or paper-based surveys. Writing clear step-by-step procedures will help you critically consider the best strategies to engage potential participants.

Data Analysis of Measures

We have finally reached an exciting step in the quantitative research process: data analysis. In this section of your dissertation, you discuss the statistical procedures you employ to analyze and interpret the data collected from the participants. Data analysis procedures utilized in a dissertation include assumptions testing, descriptive statistics, and inferential statistics (McGregor, 2018). Since you have likely completed a research statistics course, remember to reference that text and other resources to assist you with articulating the appropriate analytical procedures while writing your dissertation proposal.

Researchers clearly articulate the statistical procedures they will use for each research question, which could include a statement of rationale for the analytical approach, the name of the statistical software program, identifying applicable assumptions testing, and selecting the criteria for evaluating statistically significant results (Creswell, 2014; McGregor, 2018). Creswell (2014) advises researchers to explicitly state the independent and dependent variables for each research question. Researchers should also state and justify their intentions to conduct a post hoc statistical power analysis instead of the prior power analysis described in the "Participant and Sample Size" section. A **post hoc statistical power analysis** means the researcher will calculate the probability of rejecting a false null hypothesis after data collection using the actual sample size (Houser, 2020). Researchers report the statistical power analysis for statistically significant results to evidence trustworthiness in reporting data analysis.

Role of the Researcher

Similar to data collection methods, the role of the researcher in quantitative research corresponds with research design. The researcher's role in quantitative research is to design the study to control for threats to internal and external validity (Heppner et al., 2016). Otherwise, the role of the researcher from the positivistic paradigm advocates for unbiased engagement in the research process, whereas the researcher within the postpositivistic framework becomes one of acknowledging biases that affect the research. Quantitative researchers need to consider stating their ontological and epistemological perspectives to inform readers of the values and beliefs that informed their studies (McGregor, 2018).

Ethical Considerations

People are often the focus of quantitative research studies in social sciences. As discussed in Chapter 5 of this book, an IRB plays an essential role in assisting researchers with protecting potential study participants from harm during the research process. Most institutions have a standardized process with forms that students must follow to submit the IRB application. It is likely that the IRB at your institution will review and approve your proposed dissertation study. We will discuss one ethical issue specific to quantitative research.

A significant ethical consideration in quantitative research is the selection of instrumentation based on the population of interest. Earlier, we discussed the validity and reliability of instruments. Researchers must demonstrate awareness of the cultural relevance and psychometric soundness of instruments within a given population (Heppner et al., 2016; Houser, 2020). For example, if researchers selected an instrument written initially in Spanish for a study of English-speaking participants, they would need to reestablish validity and reliability based on the English-speaking population. The researchers would demonstrate characteristics of honesty and data integrity in the use of instrumentation. Otherwise, they may misrepresent the population and mislead readers of the study with their results—unethical practices.

Ethics in quantitative research involve protecting participants and potential consumers of research before, during, and after the study. While writing your dissertation proposal, consider following the procedures of published research based on your population. You may also find it helpful to model the reporting results of your study by modeling published research to aid you in articulating the precis, but limited application of your study findings. Overall, remember to take great care to design and report your study using established ethical standards.

Delimitations and Limitations

Delimitations and limitations play an important explanatory purpose in quantitative research. Delimitations in quantitative research articulate the predetermined scope of the study. In contrast, limitations are those facets of the study that represents weaknesses in control over threats to internal and external validity as well as the reliability of study results (McGregor, 2018). According to McGregor (2018), common delimitations are the site or location of participants, instrumentation, and treatments. She identifies limitations with quantitative research as sampling methods, measurement, inadequate statistical power, group or participation bias, and generalizability. Researchers need to state the delimitations at the beginning of their studies under a corresponding section and explain limitations after a study in the discussion section (McGregor, 2018).

Summary

Crafting and conducting quantitative research for your dissertation will take substantial planning. Each section of this chapter provided detailed information on the development and completion of a quantitative research study. Ideally, the introduction of the underlying tenets of quantitative methodology helped you solidify the appropriateness of a quantitative research design for your study. In the discussion about the role of theory, variables, and scales of measurement, you were guided to frame the research topic within the current research literature and the specific issue your study would address through the statistical analysis of the constructs of interest. The chapter also provided an overview of quantitative research designs, such as experimental, quasi-experimental, and nonexperimental. The final section of the chapter assisted you with designing a study to answer your research questions while being mindful of internal and external threats to validity and research ethics. A well-planned study has the potential to reduce the time needed to collect data, expedite the data analysis process, and result in the completion of dissertation research. Most importantly, the quantitative methodology provides you with the opportunity to contribute to your chosen discipline with statistical precision.

Online Resources

Lund Research Ltd. (2020). *Laerd Statistics*: https://statistics.laerd.com/

> *A step-by-step guide to identifying and using appropriate statistical tests with statistical software like SPSS.*

IBM SPSS. (n.d.). *Resources* https://www.ibm.com/products/spss-statistics/resources

> *User support and resources for Statistical Package for Social Sciences (SPSS).*

Statistics Solutions. (2022). *Directory of statistical analysis*: https://www.statisticssolutions.com/free-resources/directory-of-statistical-analyses/

> *A directory that explains statistical analyses with instructional tools to analyze data in SPSS.*

Stats Direct LLC. (n.d.). *Specifications*. https://www.statsdirect.com/Specifications.aspx

> *A directory of statistical terminology.*

Strata Corp LLC. (2022). *Training*. https://www.stata.com/learn/

> *User learning resources for the statistical software, including teaching resources that link to a YouTube channel.*

References

Creswell, J. W. (2014). *Research design: Qualitative, quantitative, and mixed method approaches* (4th ed.). SAGE.
Heppner, P. P., Wampold, B. E., Owen, J., Wang K. T., & Thompson, M. N. (2016). *Research design in counseling* (4th ed.). Brooks/Cole.
Houser, R. A. (2020). *Counseling and educational research: Evaluation and application* (4th ed.). SAGE.
Huck, S. W. (2008). *Reading statistics and research* (5th ed.). Pearson.
McBurney, D. H., & White, T. L. (2004). *Research methods* (6th ed.). Wadsworth.
McGregor, S. L. T. (2018). *Understanding and evaluating research*. SAGE.
Tabachnick, B. G., & Fidell, L. S. (2019). *Using multivariate statistics* (7th ed.). Pearson.

Worksheet 6.1: Quantitative Research Planner

Use the following steps to design your quantitative study. Remember, quantitative research is prescriptive. Study design is usually a linear process. You may complete these steps out of order, and you may also return to each step to refine and revise your study design. In both qualitative and quantitative, the first question is the same.

1. **Identify a research problem.**

   - What idea would you like to study? What are the key phenomena (key concepts to be explored, you can start to think about variables of interest)?

   "The topic for the study will be ..."

   _____

   - Why is this study important? What are the practical issues that led to a need for the study? Provide a compelling argument for why the topic needs to be studied. Include deficiencies or gaps in the literature.

   "This study needs to be conducted because ..."

   _____
   _____
   _____
   _____

2. **Determine what theories help explain the relationships between variables.**

   McGregor (2018) identifies exploratory, descriptive, relational, and explanatory as types of theory utilized in research inquiry. **Exploratory theory** tests or pilots a new method or instrument, whereas **descriptive theory** articulates the characteristics of the phenomena and the key variables that influence it. **Relational theory** identifies and explains relationships between variables. **Explanatory theory** finds and accounts for causal relationships. Identify theories and their types to begin to articulate possible interrelationships among them as well how they explain.

   _____
   _____
   _____

3. **Identify the type of quantitative study you will conduct with associated design.**

   - Identify which quantitative approach you will use for your study. Discuss some of the threats to internal and external validity inherent in the type of quantitative study and design.

   _____

4. **Write a purpose statement.**

    - Use the purpose statement script provided by Creswell (2014) to draft a quantitative purpose statement. If you are unsure of some aspects of your study, leave them blank and return to them later.
    - Use the following table for guidance on encoding words specific to your chosen approach:

        "The purpose of this _____ (experimental, quasi-experimental, descriptive/nonexperimental) study is (was? will be?) to test the theory of _____ that _____ (describes outcomes) or (compares? relates?) the _____ (independent variable) to _____ (dependent variable), controlling for _____ (control variables) for _____ (participants) at _____ (the research site)." (Creswell, 2014, p. 130)

    - The purpose of this quantitative study (is, will be, or was) to _____ (examine, investigate, test, assess, evaluate, describe) the _____ (influence, characteristics, relationship) of _____ (state the phenomena or phenomenon of interest) in _____ (state the target population with a specific location or setting).

5. **Write your research questions.**

    - Research questions form interrogative sentences that can begin with words like "what," "to what extent," "is," and "does" (Creswell, 2014). They also utilize similar words found in purpose statements such as "relationship," "difference," "compare," "predict," "change over time," and "describe" (Houser, 2020). Since quantitative research utilizes instruments to measure the phenomena of interest, research questions should incorporate the following: _____ (phenomena of interest) as measured by scores from _____ (instrument).
    - Write your research questions based on the guideline:

        a. _____

        b. _____

        c. _____

    State your hypothesis

    - State your hypothesis for each research question listed. State either the null alternative, or both.

        a. _____

        b. _____

        c. _____

    Describe your variables and scales of instruments (e.g., independent, dependent, or control variables and nominal, ordinal, interval or ratio scales).

6. **Collect data.**

    - Describe your methods for data collection. Include all of the following:

    Participants

    Describe the target population from whom you will collect data. The site may be included here (e.g., people diagnosed with serious mental illness receiving treatment at the X community mental health center).

    Sampling methods

    Identify the qualitative sampling strategy or strategies you will use to use to obtain a sample from the target population (e.g., select from the probability and nonprobability sampling methods. Review Table 6.2).

    Recruitment procedures

    Identify how you will solicit or recruit participants (e.g., email, social media, electronic mailing list announcement, etc.).

    Instrumentation

    List the instruments you will use to collect data. You may find it helpful to list validity and reliability information, scale of measurement, type of variable, and scoring procedures.

Data collection procedures

Describe the step-by-step process you will follow to collect data. Make sure you include a description of interventions and timing of administration of instruments.

___

7. **Analyze the data.**

   Describe the statistical procedures you will use to analyze your data. Remember specific statistical analysis are used to evaluate relationships, differences, comparisons, predictions, changes over time, and description.

___

8. **Determine the validity/measures for ensuring trustworthiness.**

   Describe how you will establish the credibility of your study (e.g., prior or post hoc statistical power analysis, reporting validity and reliability of instruments, reestablishing psychometric properties).

___

9. **Consider ethics.**

   Describe how you will ethically conduct the proposed research study in the planning, implementation, and data reporting process (e.g., IRB approval, instrumentation). In this section also identify and explain the delimitations of your study.

___

CHAPTER 7

Methodology

Your methodology will be the focus of the third chapter of your dissertation. As previously discussed in Chapters 5 and 6 of this book, both qualitative and quantitative designs are often used in dissertations. This chapter will focus on the information that you present in your third dissertation chapter, which outlines the discussion of your chosen methodology, research questions, participants, sample size, instrumentation, and analysis plans. Additionally, topics of trustworthiness, delimitations and limitations, as well as assumptions will also be explored and presented.

When introducing this third chapter of your dissertation to the readers, be sure to restate the purpose of your study, consistent with your first chapter but paraphrased here to avoid repetition. Additionally, a brief overview (a sentence or two) will be discussed regarding your research questions, restated here exactly as you presented them in chapter 1 or 2, depending on your departmental outline, and the key concepts and focus of your study. This will lead to a more thorough discussion of your methodology and your reasons for choosing to use it.

Explore how your methodology will assist in answering your research questions and how its focus will assist in gaining the insights desired. Discuss the foundational theory of your chosen methodology and how it links to both the purpose of your study and the research questions. Finally, provide a discussion of what considerations you used to determine the appropriateness of this methodology.

Considerations in Implementing Methodology

Implementation of methodology is an important aspect in designing a study and requires consideration of your chosen population and determination of sample size. Defining the population is necessary to increase replicability as well as to clarify who will be included in the study. Be sure to be consistent with your demographics from your call for participants. Consider how will you gain access to them. What approach will you use? Will you use convenience sampling or snowball sampling, or perhaps a combination of both? Did you consider random design or other sampling methods? Why did you choose this one, and why did you rule the others out? Specify your choice and reasoning and support these in the literature.

Be specific on how you will gain access to this population. Will you be using electronic mailing lists? If so, which ones? Or will you be approaching organizations to gain access to the focus population of your study? How will you contact them? Discuss your call for participants here and refer to its appendix. Be specific on how your study subjects will agree to participate, by signing an electronic informed consent or by downloading, signing, scanning, and returning one. Keep in mind that the easier the process for subjects the more likely they are to participate. For example, clicking on a link to the demographics and informed consent is much easier than having to email you to get these and send them back.

What criteria will there be to exclude a participant? For instance, what if they are personally known by the researcher or do not answer all questions? What if they don't meet demographic criteria in terms of age range, years of experience, or some other variable?

Another consideration is your sample size. How many participants do you plan to have? Why this number? Support it in the literature as well as the methodology as qualitative studies expect the number of participants to reach saturation, while quantitative sample sizes are determined by the power statistic.

Finally, consider how your participants will be represented in your findings. How will you identify them in the study? Will you do so by name or participant 1, 2, and so forth, and why? Justify your decision with the literature.

Necessary Elements of the Methodology Chapter in a Dissertation

The outline of your third dissertation chapter may vary depending on the expectations and requirements of your department and program. We provide a review of the foundational elements and considerations for their presentation in this chapter. It is strongly recommended that you use this information as supplemental to your dissertation handbook and expectations of your department, program, chair, and committee members.

Introduction

Your methodology chapter will begin like other chapters in your dissertation, with an introduction. Provide a paragraph or two summarizing the purpose of the statement and the elements that will be discussed. This chapter is often a summary of your headers throughout the chapter, so be sure to check it again upon completing the chapter to ensure it accurately reflects the chapter and information contained within it.

Research Questions

As discussed previously, your research questions guide your study. You already presented them in chapter 1 of your dissertation and present them again here in the same format. However, you also discuss various aspects of your study in detail here as well explain how you gain the answers to these questions.

Qualitative Study Considerations

If completing a qualitative study, you want to include a discussion providing an overview of your interview approach. Is it structured, unstructured, or semi-structured? Discuss the reasoning and how it will benefit your study and be sure to support this in the literature. Next, discuss how you developed your interview, which will be an attachment in your dissertation. You want to reference it as Appendix _____ and then attach it at the end of this document. Consider if your questions are overarching enough for the participant to project their perceptions? Using "how" or "what" instead of "why" helps to reduce defensiveness or justification on behalf of the respondent. Please see Chapter 5 for a more detailed discussion of the qualitative methodology and how it relates to writing chapter 3 of your dissertation.

Quantitative Study Considerations

If completing a quantitative study, you need to ensure that your questions provide both a hypothesis and null hypothesis. Refer to your dissertation manual on how this is formatted. Most often, they will be presented like in the following example:

> This study is designed to answer the following research questions (RQs).
>
> > RQ1: Are there differences in correction fatigue symptoms based on age and correctional officers' perceptions of assaults?
> >
> > RQ2: Are there significant differences in symptoms of corrections fatigue based upon tenure and gender?

Hypotheses

The following is a list of hypotheses for this study:

> Ha1: Older correctional officers (40–50+ years) who are more impacted by assaults will report higher corrections fatigue symptoms as measured by the corrections fatigue symptoms variable.
>
> Ha2: The longer the tenure of correctional officers, the more symptoms of corrections fatigue will be reported by females, as measured by the correction fatigue symptoms variable.

Research Questions and Hypotheses

At other times research questions and hypotheses may be presented together, as in the following example:

1. Are there differences in correction fatigue symptoms based on age and correctional officers' perceptions of assaults?

H_1: Older correctional officers (40–50+ years) who are more impacted by assaults will report higher corrections fatigue symptoms as measured by the corrections fatigue symptoms variable.

H_0: There is no difference in the degree of correctional fatigue symptoms based on the age of the correctional officers more impacted by assaults.

2. Are there significant differences in symptoms of corrections fatigue based on tenure and gender?

H_1: The longer the tenure of correctional officers, the more symptoms of corrections fatigue will be reported by females, as measured by the correction fatigue symptoms variable.

H_0: There is no difference in symptoms of correctional fatigue based on tenure and gender.

While writing this section, it may be useful to refer to Chapter 6 of this book to review the quantitative methodology, and it is strongly recommended to explore your dissertation handbook and consult with your chair regarding the required format of your research questions and hypotheses in your dissertation chapter.

Next, provide an overview of how you chose the instruments you used to access the data. Why did you choose this instrument over others? Discuss the reliability and validity of the scales you are using and support this decision with the literature; explain how these scales are valid with populations like yours. Details regarding the instruments will come later in your chapter, but at this juncture you want to justify your decision in using them and explain how they will best access the variables and information you are seeking.

Participant and Sample Size

Discussing your participants and sample size is important for replication. You want to provide a detailed explanation of your population and justify your sample size. You have developed your demographics to clearly identify the qualifications or roles your subjects will need to participate in your study. Clarify these details now, making this as specific as possible so that it increases replicability. Only include demographic information you specifically need for your study; for example, if age is not a variable of consideration, don't ask it. If licensure in some areas is, be sure to ask for their state and licensure number so you can verify it.

Explain reasons to not include a participant in your study. Perhaps if you knew them personally this may influence their responses or degree of honesty? Discuss how you managed data from participants who declined to answer any questions or didn't complete the interview. How would you handle it if a participant contacted you after the study was underway but not completed and they asked not to be included? Finally, be sure to review your informed consent and the IRB information.

Instrumentation

A thorough discussion of your instrumentation is necessary when explaining your methodology. You need to identify each instrument you use. This will include, but not be limited to, your call for participants, the demographic questionnaire, your informed consent document, artifacts, data storage system/devices, and data destruction systems for use after the IRB determined time frame of maintaining data. Any data analysis systems need to be discussed with justification for their use, such as NVivo for qualitative studies or SPSS for quantitative ones. Additionally, for qualitative studies you need to include your interview protocol and chosen videoconferencing platform, if applicable, along with your means of recording storage.

You want to explain, for each instrument, if they are published or produced by you and discuss the reasoning for your decision. This may include a discussion of the instrument's efficiency, cost, ease of use, or other considerations. If archival data such as legal documents or historical data are used, explain why and demonstrate they are reputable. Finally, explain why this is the best means of using this data. For example, perhaps the data provides details on variables included in suicide notes that could not otherwise be accessed.

If the instrument is published, include research to support and identify the creator, date of publication, normed population, and prior research populations it was used with. Discuss the content validity and why this is the best choice for your study and any modification(s) used. For example, will you be providing the entire survey but only using questions 1, 4, 7, and 12 for analysis? Be sure to have this reasoning based on your explained purpose and as supported in your research design.

If you are creating an instrument for your study, discuss how you created it and what literature you based it on. How was content validity established, or how will it be determined and maintained? You need to justify why this is the best instrument for your study versus well tested and published instruments.

When exploring any instrument used in your study you need to provide a full explanation of its purpose, its value to the study, justification on why it is the best instrument to use to access or process the data and support each of these decisions from the literature. You need to provide proof that you have gained approval to use any published instruments from the creators, as well as provide details on the instrument's reliability, validity, and use with similar populations or issues. Be sure to include a copy or at least a sample of the instrument, depending on copyright limitations, for your committee to review as an attachment.

Sample and Data Procedures

Data collection is discussed in this section, with a focus on how you plan to accomplish this. You want to discuss exactly how you collected your data, with a step-by-step guide to allow others to replicate your study if they so choose. How this is accomplished will depend on your chosen methodology (e.g., determining if interviews or focus groups were used to gather qualitative data versus the use of surveys or other instruments to access quantitative data).

You want to refer to the specific methodology (Chapters 5 and 6 cover these topics in detail) to ensure you are addressing each step in detail. Qualitative method studies require a discussion of your analysis plan, including any field notes or journaling you plan to do, as well as how you complete your coding and form your themes. Quantitative methods need to discuss the analysis tool as well as the confirmation of your results and how this was accomplished. Both methods require a discussion of ethical, multicultural, and social justice considerations and how each was managed as well as the safety and confidentiality of participants.

You will collect your own data for your dissertation unless using archival data. When designing your study, you considered how you will collect the data, how often you meet with the participants, and for how long. This will be discussed in detail here, along with your decisions on things like videoconferencing platforms, recording, artifacts, and data storage choices, as well as what means you will use to destroy the data upon completion of the study. A detailed discussion of your analysis systems, if applicable, will occur at this time.

You want to explore what will you do if you don't get enough participants the first time out. Electronic mailing lists with professional organizations, such as American Counseling Association, National Board of Certified Counselors, or similar organizations, reach larger groups of people who have already indicated their willingness to be contacted.

Consider the timeframe as participants are less likely to invest in over an hour. Consider if there will there be follow-ups or debriefing and justify the need for these in the literature. Remember, cast a wide net the first time to help avoid this, so consider where you can reach out to participants, and, as discussed earlier, make this process as streamlined as possible. This increases the likelihood of participation.

Be sure that each variable of data collected relates directly to one or more of your research questions. According to the APA (2020), researchers are encouraged to collect only data that directly relates to the study at hand. Do not collect information that is not directly related to your study, as this compromises the trustworthiness of the study and brings to question the purpose. For instance, if gender is not necessary to your study, don't collect that data. If your study explores the impact of some variable on gender identity, then gender identity is a logical and necessary variable for which to collect data.

A discussion of how data was analyzed, as discussed previously, will depend on your chosen methodology. Include a step-by-step data analysis and explain how outlying data or cases that don't fit the criteria or don't answer all questions are handled. A helpful hint is to keep these steps uniform for all participants, thereby reducing the impact of extraneous variables on your data and strengthens your study.

Statistical Analysis

Provide a full discussion of the analysis you plan to complete on the data. Explain the analysis type, its purpose and how it will provide insight into the research questions. Be sure that each analysis matches the types of variables explored in your study. Why did you choose one over another? For instance, perhaps a factorial MANCOVA is better suited than an ANOVA since you are exploring group differences using one categorical dependent variable with two or more categories and two or more categorical independent variables with some covariates. This "creates a linear combination of DV's to maximize mean group differences" (Mertler & Vanetta, 2013, p. 23). Such an explanation will be necessary for each analysis. Again, you are strongly encouraged to work closely with both your chair and methodologist when writing this portion of your dissertation. Chapters 5 and 6 in this book also explore this topic in more detail.

You also want to address ethical considerations, measure of trustworthiness, limitations, and delimitations, as well as assumptions as applicable. Each of these factors increases understanding of your study's design and attempts to ensure participant confidentiality and safety. Note that you will gain IRB approval and, if applicable, complete ethical trainings prior to beginning your study.

Ethical Considerations and Issues of Trustworthiness

Ethical considerations are discussed as they apply to the development and implementation of your informed consent, and you want to provide a summary of protective measures for human subjects you will use. Consider all possible ethical considerations of your study and how you address them in every stage of your design. Regarding recruitment, will incentives be used? Explain why or why not and justify this with the literature. Participant confidentiality is important both during data collection as well as in discussion of results, so outline the steps you plan to take to ensure this. Considerations of possible events, such as participant withdrawal or removal and for what reasons, as well as data collection, analysis, storage and destruction, need to be explored through the ethical consideration lens. Other possible ethical issues to be explored may include the power differential between researcher and participant as well as personal relationships that may exist between these individuals.

Measures for ensuring trustworthiness will be explored through a discussion of the steps taken to ensure internal validity (credibility) and external validity (transferability), dependability, and confirmability, as well as intra-intercoder reliability. Limitations that may occur within the study are also discussed at this juncture. What external conditions exist that may limit the execution of this study, and how will these be managed? Are there flaws in the research design? Delimitations, or the studies' boundaries based on the decision of the researcher on what to include or exclude regarding participants and variables, need to be addressed as well. Explore each and fully explain the decision-making process to justify their use in the study. What will they eliminate, and how will this enhance the current study?

Summary of the Chapter

As you wrap up this third chapter of your dissertation, you want to summarize the key topics discussed. You also want to transition to the next chapter of your dissertation, which will include the discussion of results. This section is written in the future tense as it outlines the coming chapter for the reader and highlights the information they can expect to find there.

Attachments to Include

Upon completion of your chapter, you want to include various attachments to assist the reader in being able to review detailed information related to your study. These will include your call for participants, the demographics, your informed consent, ethical trainings verification, IRB approval (once gained after your proposal), and details regarding instrumentation or other relevant information. These allow your chair, committee members, IRB, and reader to fully understand the details of each of these documents.

Call for Participants

Reaching out for participants is a form of advertising. Your call for participants will serve as an advertisement for those who may want to participate. You need to design this with the intent of clarifying who will or won't be able to participate. You want to define your population, noting specifically who will be included, making sure this is consistent with your demographics and variable.

In this section of your dissertation, outline the details of how you gain access to your research participants and what approach you use. Are you considering convenience sampling, snowball sampling, or a combination of both? Specify your choice and reasoning and be sure to support these with the literature.

Be specific on where you will reach out to the participants who meet your criteria. What electronic mailing lists or organizations will you reach out to contact your demographic? What means will be used to contact them? Personal emails or widespread notices? Be specific on how they will agree to participate.

Discuss how many participants you plan to have and explain why and how you came to this number, and support it with the literature for your chosen methodology. Explore how each will be referred to in the study. Finally, wrap up this section with a brief explanation of either saturation or sample size according to your methodology. As always, support this with the literature.

Demographics

In research, demographics can mean different things. It can be identifying information that explains who the person is, such as their age, occupation, or other factors. But for our current purposes, this is criteria that allow them to participate or exclude them from your study. This includes the variables you are studying, such as their current occupation or years of employment, but may also include aspects that may limit their participation, such as being in a personal interaction with the researcher or failing to respond to all questions of a survey or interview.

You want to consider and clearly identify the qualifications or roles your subjects will need to participate in your study. Try to make this as specific as possible so it increases replicability. It's important at this juncture to review your informed consent and the IRB information and include that information here, as applicable.

What You Need and What You Don't

Per the APA (2020), you should use bias-free language. It recommends focusing only on "relevant characteristics" or those directly related to your study, "acknowledging relevant differences that do exist" or evaluating "the meaning of the word 'difference' carefully in relation to the target population, not the dominant group" (p. 132). You want to be specific enough to provide clarity but be conscious of labels, such as age, disability, gender, and identity (APA, 2020).

Informed Consent

The informed consent allows participants to make a knowledgeable decision to be part of the study. This was discussed in Chapter 3 of this book and will be explored in more detail in Chapter 8. At this time, you want to outline that you will be using an informed consent and that you will do so in compliance with the expectations of the IRB. This consent will provide an overview of the study, its intent and purpose, and outline how choosing to participate will impact the individual both positively and, if applicable, negatively. The degree of risk will be explained, along with any compensation that may be offered. You want to make a clear statement that participants are voluntarily choosing to be part of this study and that they have the right to withdraw at any time without any fear of consequences. Reinforcing that their confidentiality will be maintained is also important. For children, their parent will consent, but the child still needs to be able to consent on the day of the interview, intervention, or participation.

It is recommended that you explain each aspect of the informed consent in detail and then provide a summary in bullet points prior to the participant signing to ensure understanding. These topics are not only mandated by IRB, but federal law as well, so be fully aware of the importance of developing a strong and honest informed consent as part of your dissertation. Take your time in developing your informed consent, review this with your chair, and provide a thorough overview of this process and its contents in this section of your dissertation.

Choosing a Platform or Means of Data Collection

Considerations for using platforms or means for collecting demographic information and the signature on your informed consent need to include thoughts of ease of use and availability of this system to your chosen population. The easier someone can complete the demographic information, the more likely they are to do so. The same can be said for signing the informed consent. Having to print something off, sign it, and then scan it back can be taxing and turn away potential participants who are busy with other aspects of their lives. Multiple emails can be burdensome and extended contacts in length or over a period may result in participants losing interest in completing the study's protocol.

Convenience needs to be a consideration as well. Do you want to have to send numerous emails hoping to get participants or contact one electronic mailing list of an organization that many of your study's population most likely are already part of? For instance, the American Counseling Association already has counselors who have signed up for their mailing lists to be in touch with others who are developing and implementing research in counseling. They have already shown an interest in research, so why not use such a list of potentially willing participants rather than try to find them on your own? And if studying counselors, you already have a population that is involved in the field and a professional organization that represents them. Win-win!

Some platforms also provide you with a summary or notice when a participant meets your inclusion criteria and signs the informed consent. You then have a ready-made list of who to schedule interviews with or send surveys to. Working smarter, not harder, is the goal of any dissertation candidate. Using technology to facilitate this is strongly recommended.

Summary

The literature review provides the foundation and rationale for your study, and your methodology chapter provides the details of your study and how you plan to answer your questions. Think of this chapter as both the ingredients list and directions of a recipe. You want to provide a detailed review of each decision you make in designing your study, both for the sake of replicability and to increase trustworthiness. Explain your decision regarding your research questions, methodological design, participants, and sample size. Include an explanation of your sampling procedures and instrumentation, as well as data analysis plan. Round out this section of your dissertation with a discussion of ethical consideration and trustworthiness, providing a sample of each document you will use, including your informed consent, demographic survey, verification of ethical training, and the like. The more details the better. Support each of these with the literature of your chosen methodology.

Online Resources

American Psychological Association. (n.d.). *General principles for reducing bias.* https://apastyle.apa.org/style-grammar-guidelines/bias-free-language/general-principles

Provides a great review of steps to take to reduce bias in writing and research.

Enago Academy. (n.d.). *How to choose the best research methodology for your study.* https://www.enago.com/academy/choose-best-research-methodology/

Helpful hints on choosing methodology to match your study's purpose and focus.

Indeed.com. (n.d.). Examples of methodology in a research paper (with definitions). 2022 https://ca.indeed.com/career-advice/career-development/examples-of-methodology

Provides a great overview of the methodology sections and defines elements of each for research papers.

References

American Psychological Association. (2020). *Publications manual of the American Psychological Association* (7th ed.). Author.

Mertler, C. A., & Vannatta, R. A. (2013). *Advanced and multivariate statistical methods* (5th ed.). Pyrczak.

Worksheet 7.1: Outline for Writing Research Questions

It is recommended that you check your dissertation handbook and discuss the preferred research question outline for your department with your chair. Following are the examples taken from this chapter with space for you to develop your study's research questions:

Research Questions

This study is designed to answer the following research questions (RQs).

> RQ1: Are there differences in correction fatigue symptoms based on age and correctional officers' perceptions of assaults?
>
> RQ2: Are there significant differences in symptoms of corrections fatigue based on tenure and gender?

Hypotheses

The following is a list of hypotheses for this study:

> Ha1: Older correctional officers (40–50+ years) who are more impacted by assaults will report higher corrections fatigue symptoms as measured by the corrections fatigue symptoms variable.
>
> Ha2: The longer the tenure of correctional officers, the more symptoms of corrections fatigue will be reported by females as measured by the correction fatigue symptoms variable.

In this example, your hypotheses are what you think will be the results. Now take some time to jot down some thoughts on possible research questions for your study using this following format:

Research Questions

This study is designed to answer the following research questions (RQs).

> RQ1:
>
> RQ2:
>
> RQ3:
>
> RQ4:

Hypotheses

The following is a list of hypotheses for this study.

> Ha1:
>
> Ha2:
>
> Ha3:
>
> Ha4:

Another way of formatting research questions is provided here:

Research Questions and Hypotheses

1. Are there differences in correction fatigue symptoms based on age and correctional officers' perceptions of assaults?

    H_1: Older correctional officers (40–50+ years) who are more impacted by assaults will report higher corrections fatigue symptoms as measured by the corrections fatigue symptoms variable.

    H_0: There is no difference in the degree of correctional fatigue symptoms based on the age of the correctional officer who are more impacted by assaults.

2. Are there significant differences in symptoms of corrections fatigue based on tenure and gender?

    H_1: The longer the tenure of correctional officers, the more symptoms of corrections fatigue will be reported by females as measured by the correction fatigue symptoms variable.

    H_0: There is no difference in symptoms of correctional fatigue based on tenure and gender.

In this example, you list your research question by the number and your hypothesis for those question by H_1, while your null hypothesis will be placed by H_0. Take some time to try your research question in this layout if you are exploring a quantitative study.

Research Questions and Hypotheses

1.
    H_1:
    H_0:

2.
    H_1:
    H_0:

3.
    H_1:
    H_0:

4.
    H_1:
    H_0:

CHAPTER 8

Dissertation Proposal Preparation

The dissertation proposal is a combination of your first three chapters of your dissertation, including your overview, your literature review, and methodology, and a presentation of your study. The dissertation committee will review the written chapters prior to the proposal defense and make note of any questions they have for you. Ensuring the proposal defense covers key aspects of the current study is imperative. Preparation of the defense is just as important as the writing of the chapters and practicing prior is a necessity.

Preparation of the Proposal

The foundational chapters of your dissertation will go through numerous revisions throughout its development. Pay close attention to the feedback you are provided. This feedback will assist you in preparing for your proposal defense as well as strengthen your proposal. Feedback indicates areas where your chair has provided a suggestion or needs clarification. Feedback will guide the evolution of your chapters but can also provide you some guidance of possible questions your committee may have for you at your proposal defense. Keeping notes of the feedback and questions posed as you receive them may assist you when you reach proposal preparation.

Formal preparation for the proposal defense will begin upon approval of your chair. Having gained approval by your chair, your first chapters, which provide the overview of the study, the complete literature review, and a full explanation of the chosen methodology, may be forwarded to your committee for an initial review. When this occurs, paying special attention to this feedback to both incorporate it as well as raise awareness of where uncertainty or additional clarity is needed. These areas of improvement may predict the questions committee members bring to the proposal defense, so awareness of this is key.

Once you have obtained and incorporated your committees' feedback into your chapters, a discussion with your chair about scheduling will occur. It is necessary to consult your dissertation handbook at this time, as you want to comply with its proposal structure. Some institutions require proposal topic or date approvals. If this applies, discuss this with your chair and follow each step of the process. Once gained, or if nonapplicable at your institution, you want to explore the **institutional review board (IRB)** requirements to ensure that you have addressed all required information. The IRB is

> a group that has been formally designated to review and monitor biomedical research involving human subjects. In accordance with FDA regulations, an IRB has the authority to approve, require modifications in (to secure approval), or disapprove research. This group review serves an important role in the protection of the rights and welfare of human research subjects. (U.S. Food and Drug Administration, n.d., para. 1)

This group is comprised of institutional faculty who are responsible to review research proposals to ensure human subjects rights and welfare are protected. Some IRBs will require both the chair and researcher to provide proof that they have completed the Collaborative Institutional Training Initiative (CITI) training. Details of this requirement will be explained in your institutional handbook.

Institutional Review Board Requirements

IRB requirements vary from institution to institution, so consulting your handbook and chair is imperative. In general, the IRB requires an application be completed once a proposal defense has been successfully completed. The IRB application is accessible from your IRB. It is recommended that you download the application and make notes of required information. This will assist you in ensuring you have addressed all necessary information for your proposal defense as well as provide you a draft for your full application.

Specific areas of concern for the IRB include a review of the **informed consent** to protect the subjects. These rights are guided by the U.S. Department of Health and Human Services's (HHS), Office for Human Research Protections. According to this office and federal regulations (45 CFR 46.116(a)), an informed consent is permission granted by a research participant indicating that they understand the purpose of the research as well as any possible risks, benefits, and compensation for their participation. The informed consent will need to include a discussion of the project, an overview of the expected time of participation and the format of the research, be it an in-person interview or completion of a battery of instruments remotely. It is important to include a discussion of the procedures and to note if any are experimental. Any risks or benefits need to be explicitly stated, along with a full explanation of the steps the researcher will take to protect the participants' confidentiality from the point they agree to participate throughout the research process, as well as after the study has concluded. Should the study include any experimental treatments or measures, or anything beyond a minimal risk, the access to compensation, medical treatment as necessary, and additional information regarding these topics needs to be provided in detail. Contact information for the researcher, their chair, and the IRB is necessary to include should a participant have questions about the research, their rights, or in case of injury. Details regarding the number of participants, costs that may be incurred by the participant because of their participation in the study, possible unforeseen side effects of participation, and any reasons a participant may be dismissed from the study also need to be included, as applicable. Finally, the informed consent needs to include that the participants are volunteering, and that participation may be halted at any point without repercussion or loss of compensation, if applicable to the study (HHS, Office for Human Research Protections, n.d.).

A useful suggestion includes having the requirements spelled out in detail, then providing a highlight of each term of participation a second time prior to the areas in which the participant will sign. This will help to ensure understanding of each item as well as a thorough review of each. Doing so may seem redundant but taking the time to provide participants details of each aspect of their participation and thoroughly developing your informed consent is foundational to a strong and ethical research project.

Compensation for research participants, although "common and, in general, acceptable practice" (U.S. Food and Drug Administration, 2018, para. 2), is not necessary and, if used, cannot be contingent on the degree of their participation. This means if they choose to withdraw from the research at any point, they still have earned their compensation. A discussion of the topic of compensation with your chair during the development of your research design is imperative, as many in academia discourage the use of compensation in doctoral dissertations. This discouragement is often based on numerous factors, including the additional cost a doctoral student will incur, as well as concern regarding the influence compensation has on recruiting participants who otherwise would not have participated (Williams & Walters, 2015). This may also raise social justice questions regarding the implication the incentive has on various socioeconomic groups or vulnerable populations (Mduluza et al., 2013; Williams & Walters, 2015). Compensation for participation needs to be critically evaluated during study development with consideration of its necessity and potential impacts on the study's population. An in-depth discussion of this topic is encouraged between the doctoral student and their chair and/or committee members.

The Proposal Process

The proposal process includes numerous moving parts, all of which need to be coordinated by the doctoral student. Considerations include gaining approval for your proposal from your chair, contacting your committee members, scheduling considerations, and preparing your presentation. Important considerations and useful hints are provided in the following section.

Gaining Approval From Your Chair

The process of gaining your chair's approval for proposal varies, as do chairs. You want to explore your dissertation handbook as well as discuss this topic with your chair. Some chairs will have you send out your draft of chapters 1–3 and related appendices to your committee for their initial review and feedback prior to scheduling the proposal. In this case, you want to send your committee these drafts in the most recently approved version by your chair. A chair may want you to send a nearly complete version and complete numerous redrafts prior to getting to this point. In this instance, when you email your committee you want to thank them for being on your committee and let them know you are requesting their initial feedback pending your upcoming proposal. Providing an idea of when you plan to propose is always helpful for your committee to plan to ensure they are available. Once you have gotten feedback from your committee and reviewed/incorporated it per your chair's recommendation, you then send out the finalized versions with your scheduled defense. We discuss that process in detail in a future section.

The process may be different for some. Some chairs may prefer that the committee see chapters 1–3 and related appendices the first time you schedule your proposal defense. If this is the scenario, work closely with your chair on redrafting your chapters until they are approved for your proposal. When this occurs, email your committee requesting a proposal date that works for them (as discussed next) and provide them with the approved versions of chapters 1–3 with related appendices upon notifying them of your proposal date. You also want to work on a draft of your IRB application to have ready for your defense date.

Contacting Your Committee Members

When contacting your committee members, keep in mind that this is a professional interaction. You want your email to be professional in tone and express your appreciation of them working with you on your research. Committee members take on dissertations as additional responsibilities to their teaching role, so respecting their time is important.

Efficiency is important when contacting your committee members. An email is appropriate to contact them with versions of your chapters and appendices but maybe burdensome when exploring availability for meetings. Discuss committee contacts with your chair and consider the purpose of the contact and allow this to dictate which means you use. Referring to any specifications outlined in your program dissertation handbook is essential to ensure you are working within the parameters expected.

Scheduling Considerations

Scheduling a proposal defense can become cumbersome through emails, as the discussion will involve numerous people responding with their availability, making it more confusing for both you and them. Streamlining this process using polling websites such as Doodle, Typeform, or Survey Monkey helps. Often these sites are available for free and allow you to provide your committee with a variety of dates and times that may work. It is important to keep in mind time zone differences if you are in an online or distance doctoral program. In these instances, be sure to clarify the time zone, usually rooted in the location of your institution, to allow committee members to accurately gauge their availability. The duration of the proposal defense will be dictated by the format of your institution's guidelines. Reviewing and discussing these expectations with your chair will be important to ensure compliance with institutional and program expectations. Worksheet 8.1 provides a checklist for considerations when working toward gaining approval from your chair and scheduling your defense with your committee members.

Preparing Your Presentation

Outlining your proposal to address all the key areas of your dissertation document completed to this point while managing a presentation within the time restraints is a balance that needs to be obtained. The defense outline may be provided by your department and/or chair, but if not it a general guideline is to address the major content areas of each chapter. Review your institutional handbook and your completed chapters, making note of your major and secondary headers. These will guide your outline.

Pertinent topics to include in your proposal are an overview/interview of your study, a discussion of the significance of your study, your problem and purpose statements, and an overview of the research questions. An overview of your literature review will also be provided in a succinct fashion. A discussion of your methodology, including a discussion of your theoretic lens and conceptual framework, as applicable, along with the research design and interpretive framework, also needs to be included.

Discussion of the chosen population, sampling procedures, sample size and justification, issues of trustworthiness, confidentiality, and processing and storage of the data will be included as well. For qualitative or mixed-measures studies, inclusion of the researcher's assumptions and role are significant topics to include. An overview of the instruments that are planned for use in the study, along with their validity and reliability measures are important inclusions for quantitative or mixed-methods designs. Finally, discussion of limitations or delimitations needs to be included prior to a summary of the project overall. Your presentation will conclude with a concise summary of the project, followed by a questions period from your committee members.

A helpful hint to consider is reviewing your prior drafts and the feedback or questions posed by your chair and committee. This will assist you in developing a checklist of areas that have previously required clarification or raised questions/interest. Reviewing these as you prepare for your dissertation will assist you in targeting prior areas in your presentation, possibly alleviating further questioning. Another preparation step will include watching prior proposal defenses, either of your peers, from your program if available, or even on the internet. This familiarizes you with both the tone of the proposal defense as well as exposes you to different styles and types of questions that may be posed.

The timing of your presentation is determined by your program. Presentation times will vary from 20 minutes to up to 30 minutes or more. Understanding the expectation is important in your presentation preparation. It is highly recommended that you practice the timing of your presentation prior to your defense so that you are confident in presenting the information in a thorough and complete way without feeling rushed or being cut off due to time limitations. Approximately 1 week prior to your proposal, send the PowerPoint along with a reminder to your committee and chair. Worksheet 8.2 provides a checklist to assist you in preparing for your dissertation proposal defense.

The Proposal Day

Your proposal dissertation proposal day has finally arrived. You have worked hard and have been practicing your timing and have your presentation ready. A helpful checklist includes double-checking your technology, including your internet connection if presenting from a distance and the share-screen process of your online platform. If presenting in person, double-checking your technology for your presentation is necessary to ensure it's working correctly and that your presentation can be viewed clearly by your committee members. Check with your chair to ensure they will take notes during your committee questions for review later. This will allow you to focus on the presentation and proposal while any recommendations are being noted for you.

Dress in professional attire and ensure that if presenting remotely your background is professional as well. Additionally, distance presentations require you to prepare your seating, which should include a table for your laptop and a chair in which you are sitting upright. Approach this with professionalism as this is the first step toward completing your dissertation and earning your PhD. This holds the weight of gaining approval for your research, but also of your professional presentation as a future leader in your field.

Prior to the start of your defense, remind yourself that you have been working on this topic for quite some time and understand your project. Take a deep breath and enjoy this moment, as it is most likely the only time in your life your will defend a dissertation proposal. This is a significant step in your dissertation process, and you have prepared. Approach this day as one of accomplishment, one you are confident in your preparation for. And remember, your committee wants you to do well.

The Defense and Considerations

It has arrived; it's show time! Keep in mind that your dissertation proposal defense is a formal step in the dissertation process. Consider the etiquette of the setting. If presenting in person or remotely, be sure to acknowledge each of your committee members and thank them for attending and their work on your research thus far. Your chair will most likely begin the dissertation by thanking the committee for attending and then transfer to you to begin your presentation. Then it's show time! Present your information as you have practiced it, professionally and at a pace that allows you to work within the time restrictions but doesn't seem rushed. Upon completion, open the presentation to questions for your committee.

Questions from your committee occur for various reasons. They may be rooted in curiosity, in seeking clarification, wanting to hear you verbally explain an aspect of your study to assess your understanding of it, or even to ensure that you have addressed all necessary aspects of the proposal defense. Field these questions as inquiries and not an indication that you missed something or were incorrect in your presentation. Answer each to the best of your ability in a professional and respectful tone and ask for clarification of the question if necessary. Becoming defensive or abrasive is a sure way to fail your proposal defense. Take a deep breath and answer the question directly and concisely, keeping in mind that your committee wants you to do well and is asking questions for their own knowledge.

After all questions have been posed and answered, you will be asked to leave the dissertation proposal defense. This may be leaving the room and waiting outside if defending in person or moving to a breakout room or exiting the online platform. During this time your committee will discuss your presentation and proposal and formulate any recommendations or amendments, as well as their final decision. The conclusion of their discussion will result in you being invited back into the discussion. Upon your return, your chair will welcome you back and inform you of the committee's decision.

Possible outcomes include a pass, pass with revisions, and a failure. A pass with revisions is the most common result and indicates that you have passed your proposal, but your committee has some recommendations or adjustments they would like to see completed in your chapters prior to your submission to IRB. This occurs to ensure that once you submit your proposal to the IRB the likelihood of approval is higher. This is a successful proposal, so celebrate this. The revisions are simply a further refinement of your proposal to strengthen it further. Graciously accept the feedback and suggestions, thank your chair for taking notes for you to discuss later, and thank your committee for their decision and recommendations.

After this outcome, you will work with your chair to incorporate the feedback and recommendations into your chapters. Once completed, the revisions will be reviewed by your chair and, if requested, your committee. Final approval of the revisions will result in your moving forward to completing your IRB application for approval. Clarify with your chair and committee the timeline for completion of these changes.

A failure at this stage will result in your committee providing feedback on what they feel needs to be revised to obtain a pass. Although difficult, maintaining a professional demeanor and remaining open to their suggestions and feedback is imperative. Take note of their suggestions and feedback, paying close attention to the areas that warranted their decision of a failure. These are the areas that will require your revision. Although no one on your committee wants to see you fail, keep in mind this decision is made to strengthen your study and best prepare you to obtain IRB approval in the future. Taking a step back for a few days from this undertaking to allow yourself to absorb this information and process your reactions is highly recommended. This allows you to reapproach your study with a clear and rational mind-set, revising as necessary and moving toward a successful proposal defense in the future.

Receiving a pass indicates that the committee feels your proposal is ready for IRB review. Remember to be gracious and thank your committee members for their work and feedback on your study. After celebrating this accomplishment, you will work with your chair to complete your IRB application and submit it, a process that is discussed in the next section.

After the Successful Defense

Congratulations! You have officially been promoted from PhD student to doctoral candidate! You have successfully defended your dissertation proposal! Once you have enjoyed this moment, the next step of the process starts, the IRB application. Which application you use will depend on the design of your study. As discussed previously in this chapter, IRB requirements vary from institution to institution, so consulting your institutional handbook and chair is imperative. Time is of the essence, as you cannot collect data until IRB approval has been granted.

These reviews are guided by the HHS, Office for Human Research Protections (n.d). According to this office and federal regulation (§46.111), IRBs must ensure research studies meet certain criteria for their approval. Figure 8.1 provides a brief overview of this process.

The HSS and regulation §46.104, exempt research includes surveys, interviews, educational tests, or observation of public behavior in which the researcher maintains the subject's confidentiality and that would not place the subject at risk for any liability or damage to their public image if their identity were ascertained. This regulation further stipulates that the subjects are not exposed to harmful, invasive interventions that would impact them long-term. Under the statue §46.110, an expedited review may be used for specific types of research where human subjects are presented with risks to subjects that do not exceed minimal levels or if prior approved research requires minor changes. An expedited review would need to meet the criteria of the exempt review but includes use of drugs/medical devices, collection of biological specimens or the use of biological testing, secondary analysis of data collected for nonresearch purposes or use of archival data containing audio or visual recordings, or archival data regarding aspects of human behavior such as thoughts, interpersonal communication, interviews, oral history, or evaluations of any kind.

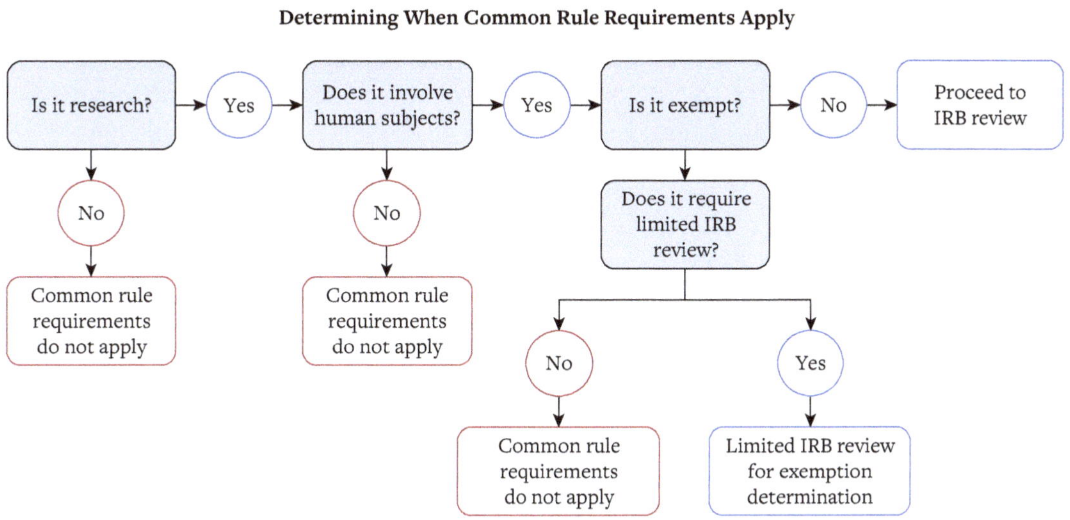

Determining When Common Rule Requirements Apply

FIGURE 8.1 Overview of IRB process.

Full IRB reviews are used for any study not meeting the criteria for either the exempt or expeditated review. If studies remain active for extended periods of time for follow up with subjects, a continued review may also be required (HHS, Office for Human Research Protections, n.d.). Should a new intervention or change in procedure, including the call for participants, informed consent, criteria, or participation occur, an amended IRB review may be necessary. Please consult with both your institution's IRB and chair regarding these instances.

Summary

Preparing for your dissertation proposal defense is a significant moment in your academic career and a milestone in your progression toward completing your PhD. Working closely with your chair throughout chapter revisions and the development of your appendices is imperative. Your program's dissertation guide will provide invaluable information on the required content and format. Your institution's IRB will provide necessary information to guide the development of your informed consent to ensure trustworthiness and participant confidentiality.

Preparation for your proposal defense begins with your chapters and related appendices, which provide the foundation for your presentation. Your dissertation handbook will outline proposal defense specifics regarding format and time restrictions. Completion of the CITI training ensures you are prepared as a researcher to work with human subjects. Consultation with your chair throughout this phase of preparation is essential to ensure that you are meeting both institutional and IRB requirements.

On the day of your defense try to enjoy the moment and experience while professionally presenting the rationalization for your study. Your committee is there to ensure you meet IRB requirements, but also to encourage your and strengthen your study with any suggestions. Reminding yourself that your committee is offering feedback to enhance your study will allow you to accept their feedback both graciously and openly.

After successfully defending your proposal, your next major task is to gain IRB approval. This is accomplished through consultation with your chair and a review of the IRB applications and understanding the different requirements to meet the criteria of an exempt, expedited, full IRB review. Through diligent assessment of each application criteria, you will find the best fit for your study, and IRB approval is then just a step away. Upon receiving IRB approval, you move into data collection, which will be discussed in the next chapter.

Online Resources

The Collaborative Institutional Training Initiative. (CITI Program) (n.d.). *About.* https://about.citiprogram.org/

The Collaborative Institutional Training Initiative. (CITI Program) (n.d.). *QA/QI: Human Subject Research.* https://about.citiprogram.org/course/qa-qi-human-subjects-research/

> *Both provide various trainings for students and faculty on research, ethics, and standards trainings.*

Dummies. (n.d.). *How to plan your dissertation proposal.* https://www.dummies.com/education/college/how-to-plan-your-dissertation-proposal/

> *Helpful hints to assist in outlining your proposal and consideration of necessary aspects.*

Tippens, S. (2020, August 20). *Dissertation proposal defense: 12 tips for effective preparation.* Beyond PhD Coaching. https://www.beyondphdcoaching.com/dissertation/dissertation-proposal-defense/

> *Provides helpful suggestions for preparing for the dissertation proposal defense, including suggestions for both before and during your defense.*

U.S. Department of Health and Human Services, Office for Human Research Protections. (n.d.). *2018 requirements (2018 Common Rule), federal regulations (45 CFR 46.116(a)).* https://www.hhs.gov/ohrp/regulations-and-policy/regulations/45-cfr-46/revised-common-rule-regulatory-text/index.html#46.116

> *Provides a thorough review of the requirements for human subjects and specific details of necessary requirements of the informed consent and other guidance for conducting research with human subjects.*

U.S. Department of Health and Human Services, Office for Human Research Protections. (n.d.). *Lesson 2: What is human subjects research?* https://www.hhs.gov/ohrp/education-and-outreach/online-education/human-research-protection-training/lesson-2-what-is-human-subjects-research/index.html

> *Provides a review of human subject research and the levels of IRB approval.*

U. S. Food and Drug Administration. (2018, January). *Payment and reimbursement to research subjects: Guidance for institutional review boards and clinical investigators.* https://www.fda.gov/regulatory-information/search-fda-guidance-documents/payment-and-reimbursement-research-subjects

> *Provides guidance for researchers regarding payment and reimbursement for participants in research.*

References

Mduluza, T., Midzi, N., Duruza, D., & Ndebele, P. (2013). Study participants incentives, compensation and reimbursement in resource-constrained settings. *BMC Medical Ethics, 14*(S1), S4–S4. https://doi.org/10.1186/1472-6939-14-S1-S4

U.S. Department of Health and Human Services, Office for Human Research Protections. (n.d.). *2018 requirements (2018 Common Rule), federal regulations (45 CFR 46.116(a))*. https://www.hhs.gov/ohrp/regulations-and-policy/regulations/45-cfr-46/revised-common-rule-regulatory-text/index.html#46.116

U.S. Food and Drug Administration. (n.d.). *Institutional review boards (IRBs) and protection of human subjects in clinical trials*. https://www.fda.gov/about-fda/center-drug-evaluation-and-research-cder/institutional-review-boards-irbs-and-protection-human-subjects-clinical-trials

U.S. Food and Drug Administration. (2018, January). *Payment and reimbursement to research subjects: Guidance for institutional review boards and clinical investigators*. https://www.fda.gov/regulatory-information/search-fda-guidance-documents/payment-and-reimbursement-research-subjects

Williams, E. P., & Walter, J. K. (2015). When does the amount we pay research participants become "undue influence"? *AMA Journal of Ethics, 17*(12), 1116–1121. https://doi.org/10.1001/journalofethics.2015.17.12.ecas2-1512

Worksheet 8.1: Checklist for the Proposal Process

CONSIDERATION	STEPS TAKEN TO ACCOMPLISH THIS		DATE COMPLETED
Gaining approval for your proposal from your chair	Provided finalized versions of chapters 1–3 with all appendices to your chair for review		
	Gained final approval of chapters 1–3 with all appendices from your chair		
	Discussed timeframe of proposal with chair; completed any necessary paperwork to obtain this per your institutional requirements		
	(i.e., dissertation proposal topic approval, dissertation proposal date approval, etc.)		
	Agreed on workable proposal defense date range with chair		
Contacting your committee	Discuss with chair who will contact the committee members re: proposal date		
	If dissertation chair is contacting committee members	Provide dates/times and any additional details to chair	
	If you are responsible for contacting committee members	Choose method of contact	
		Provide a range of dates and times available for the proposal	
		Confirm chosen date that works for all committee members	
		Send notice of location of defense or platform link if defending remotely	

Worksheet 8.2: Important Items to Include in Your Presentation

ITEM	INFORMATION TO INCLUDE	SLIDE NUMBER OF PRESENTATION
Overview of study		
Significance of study		
Problem statement		
Purpose statement		
Research questions		
Literature review overview		
Methodology overview		
Theoretic lens		
Conceptual framework (as applicable)		
Research design		
Interpretive framework		
Population		
Sampling procedures		
Sample size and justifications		
Issues of trustworthiness		
Confidentiality		
Instrumentation (reliability and validity for quantitative and mixed-methods designs)		
Data processing		
Data storage		
Limitations and delimitations		
Summary of project		
Questions from committee		

Credit

Fig. 8.1: Source: https://www.hhs.gov/ohrp/education-and-outreach/online-education/human-research-protection-training/lesson-2-what-is-human-subjects-research/index.html.

PART IV

Data Collection and Beyond

CHAPTER 9

Data Collection and Processing

In the fourth chapter of your dissertation, you focus on writing the details of how you collected your data and the analysis of this. You provide a thorough discussion of your methodology and explore the results of your study. Chapter 7 of this book provides an overview to each of the elements you will provide a detailed discussion of at this juncture. A significant point to consider is that your tense will now be past when discussing your study, as you have completed it. If you have not done so already, spend some time changing your first three chapters to past tense as well, since it was written in the future tense.

Call for Participants

You previously discussed your call for participants in detail in chapter 3 of your dissertation. Here, you provide a brief overview of this, highlighting the definition of your population and how you gained access to them. Review for the reader the approach you used, specifying your choice and your reasoning, which should be rooted in the literature.

Provide the reader with a review of the organization or electronic mailing lists used to gain your participants, as well as with an overview of the steps taken to introduce your study to the participants and how they agreed to participate. Remind the reader of the total number of participants and the reasoning for this, justified by the literature. There is no need to go into a long discussion; you already provided that in the prior chapter. Here, you just need a review to set the stage for the discussion of the results. Wrap up your discussion with an overview of how your participants will be identified in the study and a review of saturation and sample size determination.

Demographics

You previously discussed your demographics, or the criteria by which you chose the qualifications for participants to be part of your study. Here, you provide a review of this information.

Be sure to include an explanation of criteria for inclusion or exclusion. Review your informed consent and the necessary information regarding the IRB, and be sure to include that information here, as applicable.

You also want to provide a brief discussion of your demographic variables as they relate to your study. As discussed in Chapter 7 of this book, you already considered and evaluated the information for including or excluding, based on the relation of these elements to your study and the need to gather that specific information. Highlight these choices here once more before moving on to the next section.

Informed Consent

Your informed consent was previously developed and approved prior to your IRB endorsement of your study. At this juncture, review how your informed consent was accessed and completed by the participants and if any subjects chose to withdraw from the study. Keep in mind that you have already discussed this in detail, so provide a brief overview of the process for the reader to reflect on the foundational aspects of your study.

Gathering Data

In your current writing of your dissertation's fourth chapter, you begin to provide new information to the reader. When exploring how you gathered the data, provide a thorough discussion of what you did. Walk the reader through the steps you took from when a participant signed the informed consent to be part of your study. Highlight your use of HIPPA-compliance platforms to contact them. Did you use an encrypted email provider or some other platform? How did you protect their confidentiality?

How did you schedule times to meet with them for qualitative interviews or provide them with the instruments for quantitative evaluations? Once you started collecting the data, how did you store it? Be specific on how it was stored, where, who had access to it, and why these choices were made. How long will the data be maintained? Note the IRB requirements for this. Once your study is completed and data disposal is permitted, how will this be performed and by whom? Provide a detailed explanation of each step of this process, noting any professional data disposal services you may have chosen to employ.

Processing the Data

Next will turn your writing to focusing on the processing of the data. Data analysis, as discussed in Chapters 5, 6, and 7 of this book, depends on your chosen methodology. Both methodologies require a detailed discussion of the steps taken in managing and analyzing your data.

Qualitative studies need to include a discussion of your data analysis plan. How did you initially analyze your data, and what were your initial findings? Provide an overview of your coding procedures, offering a detailed explanation of any data you chose to exclude and why. Provide a summary of your initial findings.

Next, explore your reflexive self-analysis. Did you use bracketing or bridling? Heuristic analysis or self-reflection? Did you use theoretical memos or field notes? Did you use participant reviews, peer reviews, or other auditors? Discuss how each of these were used in your study and how they contributed to your initial data analysis.

Outline how you refined your themes and developed your categories. Part of this discussion will include your organization the themes and codes. Support these with rich, thick quotes highlighting each theme. Your connection of codes to themes should be obvious and the connection of your participant quotes evident.

Quantitative studies will provide a discussion of the participant demographics, sample size, and discussion of how data was cleaned and screened. Any missing data, along with outliers, will be addressed and how each was handled will be explored. Discuss in detail how the distribution of your data was normalized and how any variables that failed to meet this assumption were managed. Any post hoc analysis also needs to be addressed at this time.

Each hypothesis will be presented along with the specific analysis performed that led to the study's results. Provide a detailed explanation of if the hypothesis was accepted or rejected and the reasoning for this, supported by the statistical data.

Provide a discussion of how pre- and post-scores on the dependent variable differ between groups, treatment, or other variables with a thorough explanation of the associated statistical analysis discussed. Provide results related to reliability and validity as well as any related analysis of the study's dependent variables. Including a discussion of internal consistency measures is necessary as well.

Provide a detailed discussion of your data analysis. Present each statistical test you conducted in table form with a full discussion of the findings. Discuss covariates or confounding variables as well as your interpretation of results, considering confidence internals, odds ratios, and the like. Review each hypothesis this way, providing the statistical support of tables and figure for each.

This chapter wraps up with a summary of your results, not by rewriting them but highlighting the findings. You then conclude with a paragraph that leads to the final chapter, in which you discuss the implications of your study for your field and how your findings support or contradict the established literature. Explore the Chapter 10 of this book to assist you in a detailed discussion of presenting your results.

Summary

An overview of your study, in which you remind the reader of the details of who your participants are, how you gained access to them and protected their confidentiality and safety, as well as the inclusion/exclusion criteria for their participation, is essential. A discussion of your data analysis process will be provided, walking the reader step by step through this. A detailed review supports not only understanding but trustworthiness as it allows for replication. Results are provided and explained in detail to allow the reader to fully understand and appreciate your work. The presentation of results are explored more in the next chapter of this book.

Online Resources

Dillon. L. (n.d.). *How to present quantitative & qualitative data together in reporting: Learn how to effectively present qualitative and quantitative data in your management reports, transforming them into the* most valuable tools in your organization. ClearPoint Strategy. https://www.clearpointstrategy.com/qualitative-and-quantitative-data/

>A quick read on how to present results from both methodologies.

NMBU. (n.d.). *Writing about quantitative results*. https://nmbu.instructure.com/courses/2280/pages/writing-about-quantitative-results?module_item_id=15798

>Provides an overview of the process of presenting quantitative results from research.

Royal Geographic Society. (n.d.). *A guide to presenting qualitative data*. https://www.rgs.org/CMSPages/GetFile.aspx?nodeguid=aa63d52d-929f-4e8d-a6b7-5d2019d147d3&lang=en-GB

>A useful guide with examples of how to present qualitative data in both written and verbal form.

Studysmarter.com. (n.d.). *Presentation of quantitative data*. https://www.studysmarter.de/en/explanations/psychology/data-handling-and-analysis/presentation-of-quantitative-data/

>Provides a discussion of how to present qualitative data from research.

Verdinelli, S., & Scagnoli, N. I. (2013). Data display in qualitative research. *International Journal of Qualitative Research, 12*(1), 359–381. https://journals.sagepub.com/doi/pdf/10.1177/160940691301200117

>Provides a detailed discussion of how to display data in qualitative research with examples and useful resources.

Worksheet 9.1: Example of Qualitative Results

Qualitative results may be written differently as they strive to have the voice of the participants be heard, so two examples are provided here:

Being Viewed as Different From Civilians

The category being viewed as different from civilians is included within the theme of feeling disconnected. This theme is important to the overall theory of identity development for veteran women because the feelings of disconnection play a role in all four stages of identity development. For this category, 18 women endorsed feeling disconnected by being viewed as different from civilians. For instance, McKenzie provided an example of how work ethic is different in the civilian sector within the theme of watching and learning from civilians. McKenzie shared, "I get up every morning and I'll study for an exam, and I see these kids just like yeah, I wear pajamas to school." Her example also illustrates how she is viewed as different from civilians. Hammond (2016) confirms the disconnection between civilians and veterans within a college setting, elaborating that veterans see civilian students as immature, less disciplined, lacking an appreciation for their college education (Hammond, 2016). Veterans were distracted by their frustrations about their civilian peers, feeling as if veterans had earned their education with blood, sweat, and tears, whereas civilians were less appreciative (Hammond, 2016), not unlike McKenzie feeling frustrated that her peers showed up to school in pajamas.

In a more general sense, veteran women also felt different from civilian women. Greer (2020) stated that veteran women often feel like they are not veteran enough or woman enough. Veterans became frustrated when civilian women would ask questions about why veteran women behaved the way they do, using words like militant to describe veteran women (Greer, 2020). Charlie exemplified how she did not feel woman enough when she stated, "I don't feel like I meet the expectation of a regular female in today's society." Charlie's example is also found in the theme of watching and learning from civilians (category: observing femininity and ways of socializing), illustrating another example of how feeling disconnected is pervasive within various aspects of the civilian identity development of veteran women (pp. 170–171).

Second Example

Kentucky school counselors have the ASCA National Model to guide their efforts in creating a comprehensive school counseling program, as well as the Kentucky Framework of Best Practices for School Counselors. Holly acknowledged how "Kentucky is focused on the standards of practice and few conferences or meetings have anything to do with the ASCA Model." May argued that the Kentucky Framework of Best Practices "couldn't have been written without the ASCA Model." Looking beyond specific models, standards, and both professional organization and

Kimberly Hardy, Excerpt from "Process of Identity Development among Women Veterans Who Are Transitioning from Military to Civilian Life," pp. 170-171. Copyright © 2022 by Kimberly Hardy. Reprinted with permission.

Whitney Peay, Excerpt from "Bridging the Gap: School Counselors Experiences on the Implementation of the ASCA National Model," pp. 64-66. Copyright © 2020 by Whitney Peay. Reprinted with permission.

identity is crucial. Sara-Jean stated what many school counselors in this study communicated: "What you have and what you're working towards all connects."

As school counselors bring together the resources present to ultimately meet the goals of a comprehensive school counseling program, both program and individual evaluation must occur. Throughout the interviews, the school counselors discussed how students are supported academically, social emotionally, in the area of mental health, and postgraduation needs. The majority of participating school counselors discussed the themes of collaboration, partnership, and even disconnect regarding how students are supported in all the above areas. The educational system has long focused on improving academic standards, student support, and postgraduation success (Cinotti, 2014). For decades administration and staff have worked collaboratively to identify "at-risk" students from a tiered perspective. Holly explained academically they have a "pretty serious intervention time." Such interventions include before school homework assistance, testing and assessments, hiring multiple interventionists within districts, and all school personnel working together. Participating school counselors all agree the profession of school counseling and the academic world has had to evolve because of the COVID-19 pandemic.

Not only are school counselors like Holly seeing that "a lot of kids have fallen through the cracks academically with COVID" but how the need is increasing for both SEL and mental health supports within the school building. Sara-Jean stated, "Social emotional learning is a big push right now." School counselors collectively acknowledged the need for SEL to be incorporated within all academic areas. Alice discussed how teachers utilize SEL "as a collaborative effort in the classroom to drive the importance of the academic side of things and SEL curriculum." It is with this effort that Alice reported their school is "trying to utilize every chance and opportunity we get to infuse SEL into our daily routines." Both SEL and mental health supports were commonly determined through a tiered approach and the use of SEL or mental health screeners such as Terrace Metrics, the Student Risk Screening Scale (SRSS), and Panorama (pp. 64–66).

Example of Quantitative Results

Following is the layout for a discussion of quantitative results, with an example provided afterward.

Hypothesis Testing
Variable on Population (Hypothesis 1)

It was hypothesized the population would report what was measured by the variable. Data were screened to ensure the assumptions of chosen analysis (i.e., factorial ANOVA [independence of observations, interval data of the dependent variable, normality, homoscedasticity, and absence of multicollinearity]) were fulfilled. It contained # independent type-level variables (i.e., two independent nominal-level variables [A and B]) and one type of variable (i.e., interval-dependent variable [corrections fatigue symptom intensity]). Outliers were significant/insignificant, being what % of the sample, and did/did not need to be eliminated based on what (their insignificance). A specific measure (i.e., 7×3 ANOVA) was conducted to investigate the relationship between what and what. A summary of the results is presented in Table #. Specific statistics explained their meaning. This fails to support/supports the hypothesis that population with variable would report what as measured by variable, as explanation.

Table #

Figure #

Example

The example is taken from the dissertation noted here:

Mikolon, T. M. (2017). The impact of prison social climate on corrections fatigue syndrome [Doctoral dissertation] (Publication No. 10281958). ProQuest Dissertations & Theses Global.

Impact of Assaults Age of Correctional Officer (Hypothesis 1)

It was hypothesized that older correctional officers (age 40+) who identify as being most bothered by assaults would report higher corrections fatigue symptoms as measured by the corrections fatigue symptom variable. Data were screened to ensure the assumptions of factorial ANOVA (independence of observations, interval data of the dependent variable, normality, homoscedasticity, and absence of multicollinearity) were fulfilled. It contained two independent nominal-level variables (perception of assaults and age) and one interval dependent variable (corrections fatigue symptom intensity). Outliers were insignificant, being less than 5% of the sample, and did not need to be eliminated based on their insignificance.

7 × 3 ANOVA was conducted to investigate the relationship between the intensity of corrections fatigue symptoms and correctional officer perception of assaults and age. A summary of the results is presented in Table 9.1. Although interaction between perception of assaults and age group was not statistically significant, $F(12, 4346) = 1.225$, $p = .259$, Figure 9.1 does reveal some interaction. Main effects reveal that corrections fatigue symptom intensity was significantly different among correctional officers based on their perception of assaults, $F(6, 4346) = 35.306$, $p < .001$ and by age group, $F(2, 4346) = 13.585$, $p < .001$. Estimates of effect size reveal low

TABLE 9.1 Between Subjects Effects – Assaults

SOURCE	TYPE III SUM OF SQUARES	DF	MS	F	SIG.
Corrected Model	257.163ª	20	12.858	19.705	.000
Intercept	11158.868	1	11158.868	17100.512	.000
BotheredAssaults	138.231	6	23.039	35.306	.000
Age	17.730	2	8.865	13.585	.000
BotheredAssaults * Age	9.593	12	.799	1.225	.259
Error	2835.964	4346	.653		
Total	25878.142	4367			
Corrected Total	3093.127	4366			

a. $R^2 = .083$ (Adjusted $R^2 = .079$)
b. Computed using alpha = .05

strength in associations. Levene's test for equality of variances was significant, $F(20, 4346) = 4.829$, $p < .001$, and Bonferroni's post hoc test was conducted to determine which 64 groups were significantly different in corrections fatigue symptom intensity. Results reveal that those who are strongly not bothered or not bothered by the frequency with which inmates have used physical force against staff are significantly different from all other group perceptions of the impact of assault against staff. There was also a significance difference between the 20–29-year-old age group and the other older age groups, but none exist between the two older age groups. Specifically, the 20- to 29-year-old age group had lower corrections fatigue symptom intensity than the older age groups. This fails to support the hypothesis that older correctional officers (40–50 years+) who are more impacted by assaults would report higher corrections fatigue symptoms as measured by the corrections fatigue symptoms variable, as those ages 30–39 had the highest reported corrections fatigue symptom intensity when most impacted by their perception of assaults.

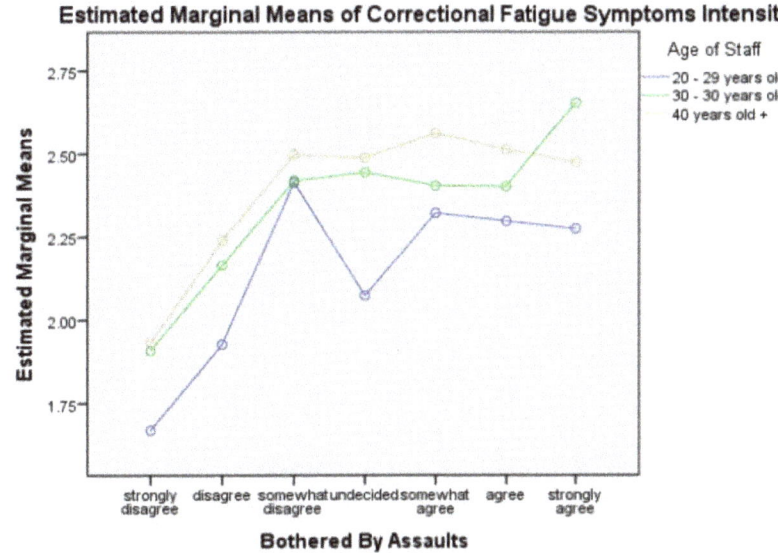

FIGURE 9.1 Estimated marginal means –Assaults.

CHAPTER 10

Results

You have identified the goal of your study, developed your research questions to target your intended variables, developed your conceptual and theoretic framework, and determined the most appropriate means of gathering the data. You have worked diligently, collected all data, and completed the appropriate analysis based on the chosen methodology. Your hard work has placed the finish line within your sight, and now you need to present your findings.

In chapter 4 of your dissertation, you present the results of your study through a discussion of your methodology and findings. You'll start your chapter with a brief introduction that highlights the problem statement, purpose, methodology, and data collection procedures. A brief discussion of the data analysis will be provided, as well as an overview of the coming sections of the chapter.

Presenting the Data Analysis

When presenting the data analysis, it is imperative that you provide a review of your data collection procedures, including a brief discussion of your population and a restatement of your research questions. Qualitative and quantitative methodologies will vary on how the data is presented; thus, a discussion of each will be provided. Regardless of methodology, a discussion of the analysis is essential. Both methodologies were discussed in detail in Chapters 6 and 7 of this textbook.

Qualitative Data Analysis Presentation

When presenting qualitive data analysis, include a review of all analyses performed. As explored in Chapter 5, you want to provide a summary of each step you took in handling the data and analyzing it. A thorough discussion increases replicability, thereby increasing transparency through a presentation of the "data, analysis, methods, and interpretive choices" (Moravcsik, 2020, p. 2). Discuss the steps to ensure trustworthiness and provide a brief discussion on qualitative theory, followed by the steps taken to analyze the data and the resulting initial findings, followed by a discussion of the coding procedures and any data you chose not to include and your justification. Discuss your theoretical framework, including any journaling, bracketing, bridling, or heuristic analysis completed, as well as any field notes you may have compiled, and how each impacted the data analysis. If you used data-checking methods with your participants, discuss that process in detail, as well as if you used any outside sources such as peers to assist in the identification of repetitive words, resulting codes, categories, or themes. Providing thick, rich quotes from participants to support your identified themes is strongly recommended, as it brings the results to life. Upon completing a thorough discussion of each of these aspects, the chapter will conclude with a summary. The reader will be provided with a summary of all results and a brief introduction into the final chapter of the dissertation. Worksheet 10.1 provides a useful checklist for ensuring you cover all necessary aspects of reporting your results.

Quantitative Data Analysis Presentation

When presenting quantitative data, providing a review of all analyses performed is necessary, including participant demographics, sample size, post hoc analysis power determinations, data collection, and the handling of missing or outlying data. A review of your descriptive analysis, referencing relevant tables or figures, is included in both your chapter and presentation. Each hypothesis is then discussed individually and presented on their own slide. Necessary information includes a discussion of the outliers and their management, the determination of normality and its impact on the variables, and an evaluation of pre- and post-score impact on the dependent variable for each hypothesis. Any relevant test completed to determine these needs to be explained thoroughly as well. Discussing the validity and reliability of the measures needs to be thorough yet concise and should include all the pertinent information outlined in Chapter 6.

An explanation of the analysis completed, with a restatement of the purpose of the analysis, to determine association or correlation as well as if subjects are repeatedly measured or different subjects are used for each needs to be included (Samuels, 2020). A discussion of the effect size as well as the null hypothesis testing with an explanation of the significance value should also be included, with attention to internal consistency estimates. Confirmation of your results by a qualified statistician is highly recommended, and if used needs to be noted. This provides validation of your results, and credit should be given to your statistician who assisted in this. Noting that they were confirmed by an outside statistician will suffice; mentioning the statistician in your acknowledgments is fitting.

A thorough discussion of hypothesis testing will be provided. Each hypothesis will be explained, independent and dependent variables will be identified, and the analysis performed will be discussed. Significance will be explored through a detailed explanation of the statistics completed, and an explanation of the results will be provided. This will be repeated for each hypothesis individually. Relevant tables and figures will be referenced and included in appendices.

Consistent with prior chapters in your dissertation, this chapter will conclude with a summary. The reader will be provided with a summary of all results and a brief introduction to the final chapter of the dissertation, regardless of chosen methodology. A checklist for ensuring you cover all necessary aspects of reporting your results is provided in Worksheet 10.2.

Notes on Formatting

The professional writing of your field will determine the formatting for your dissertation. You need to be sure you are familiar with the writing style and the expectations for your document. As with any professional writing, you want to use the correct level of headings to organize your data, which assist the reader in focusing on each question and the correlated results. The use of tables and figures, as dictated and necessitated by your chosen methodology, need to be formatted according to the writing style of your chosen field and placed in identified appendices rather than in the chapter itself. Special attention needs to be invested at this point, as the formatting of your data presentation needs to be consistent with dissertation expectations as well as to represent your findings in a comprehensible and professional manner.

Considerations for the Presentation of Results

When presenting your results during your defense, you want to provide clear and concise information. Chapter 12 of this textbook discusses preparing for your defense; here we explore just the sections of your presentation of your findings. Regardless of methodology, you want to provide a summary of your initial analysis and findings, as well as your coding procedures, self-analysis techniques, and fact-checking, if using qualitative methodology. Highlight the process you used to refine your themes, providing an overview of how you organized and ultimately determined the saturation of the data, codes, themes, and categories. These can be summarized in one or two slides, understanding that your committee has read the chapter and your findings. Much of your time for this chapter will be spent on presenting the themes you found and providing examples of thick, rich quotes that provide support for your codes, themes, and categories.

When presenting quantitative results, this section of your presentation begins with identification of the independent and dependent variables, a discussion of the relationship between variables, and your participant demographics. An overview of your sample size and justification will be provided, as well a summary of your data collection process, keeping in mind your committee has read your chapter and the details regarding these aspects of your study. An overview of the handling of missing data and outliers will lead to an explanation of assumptions of normality, as well as that of construct reliability and validity and pre- and post-score analysis as they relate to the relationship between the independent and dependent variables. Most of your time will be spent discussing each hypothesis in detail, commenting on the analysis used and the determination of significance. Each hypothesis is presented on its own slide, with relevant tables and figures included on subsequent slides.

Summary

Completing the analysis of your data is a significant step forward toward completion of your PhD dissertation, but the presentation of it is important as it allow others to understand the fruits of your labor. When presenting your results, consideration of the methodology used is important, as it will dictate the steps of analysis used; both qualitative and quantitative will be discussed in this chapter of your dissertation. Providing the reader with a thorough understanding of each step of analysis increases transparency and replicability, which increase the validity of the results. Spending time at this pivotal point of your writing is important, as you want to be sure your results are clear and concise and that you use figure and tables as needed to support the findings and increase understanding. Close attention needs to be paid to formatting, as new aspects of writing present themselves at this juncture. The reader's comprehension is used to guide the discussion of your results, and a final summary of findings will logically lead them to the final chapter of your dissertation.

Online Resources

Grad Coach. (n.d.). *Quantitative data analysis 101 tutorial: Statistics explained simply + examples*. https://www.youtube.com/watch?v=EUeQRE5UJpg&list=RDCMUCHac4-z13FBSD-ue8Jt40Eg&start_radio=1&rv=EUeQRE5UJpg&t=0

> *A 28-minute video discussing statistics and analysis of data.*

Humans of Data. (2018, September). *Your guide to qualitative and quantitative data analysis methods*. https://humansofdata.atlan.com/2018/09/qualitative-quantitative-data-analysis-methods/

> *Provides a great overview of both qualitative and quantitative analysis, including a review of data organization, editing, coding, and descriptive statistics as well as developing research objectives and finding themes.*

National Institute for Children's Health Quality. (2021, April). *Qualitative data collection: 7 things researchers need to know to get it right*. https://www.nichq.org/insight/qualitative-data-analysis-7-things-researchers-need-know-get-it-right

> *Provides a concise review of qualitative research methodology.*

Pell Institute and Pathways to Connect Network. (n.d.). *Evaluation toolkit: Evaluation guide*. http://toolkit.pellinstitute.org/evaluation-guide/collect-data/

> *Provides a great overview of the process of collecting data, linking your questions to your methodology, and determining sample size, as well as analysis and numerous resources.*

Question Pro. (n.d.). *Quantitative data: Definition, types, analysis and examples*. https://www.questionpro.com/blog/quantitative-data/

> *Provides a discussion of quantitative research, including a review of collection methods, analysis, and the strengths and weakness of using quantitative data.*

Samuels, P. (2020, April). *A really simple guide to quantitative data analysis*. https://www.researchgate.net/publication/340838762_A_Really_Simple_Guide_to_Quantitative_Data_Analysis

> *A concise guide to quantitative data analysis touching on the definition of quantitative analysis and providing useful steps for data analysis.*

Wong, L. (2008). Data analysis in qualitative research: A brief guide to using NVivo. *Malaysian Family Physician: The Official Journal of the Academy of Family Physicians of Malaysia, 3*(1), 14–20. https://www.ncbi.nlm.nih.gov/pmc/articles/PMC4267019/

> *A great article outlining the use of NVivo for qualitative data analysis.*

References

Moravcsik, A. (2020). *Transparency in qualitative research*. SAGE Research Methods. https://www.princeton.edu/~amoravcs/library/TransparencyinQualitativeResearch.pdf

Samuels, P. (2020, April). *A really simple guide to quantitative data analysis*. https://www.researchgate.net/publication/340838762_A_Really_Simple_Guide_to_Quantitative_Data_Analysis

Worksheet 10.1: Qualitative Research Considerations

CONSIDERATION	NOTES	DATE COMPLETED
Discussion of initial analysis		
Discussion of initial findings		
Discussion of coding procedures		
Discussion of data not included, if applicable, and reasoning to justify this		
Discussion of self-analysis used, with support of it in your theoretic framework		
Discussion of field notes or theoretic memos and their relation to data analysis		
Discussion of fact checking with participants, if applicable		
Discussion of outside reviewers, if applicable		
Discussion of theme refinement: themes; categories		
Discussion of organization of codes, themes, and categories		
Thick, rich quotes provided to support codes, themes, and categories		
A summary of findings		

Worksheet 10.2: Quantitative Considerations

CONSIDERATION	NOTES	DATE COMPLETED
Identification of independent and dependent variables		
Discussion of relationship between variables		
Participant demographics explored		
Sample size explained and justification provided		
Post hoc power discussed and justification provided		
Data collection discussed		
Handling of missing data discussed		
Handling of outliers discussed		
Explanation of normality assumptions provided		
Discussion of construct validity and reliability provided		
Discussion of independent and dependent variables provided with consideration of pre- and post-score analysis and resulting relationship or differences explained		
For each hypothesis: Identify the independent and dependent variable		
For each hypothesis Discuss the specific analysis completed		
For each hypothesis Note statistical significance and how it was determined		

(continued)

CONSIDERATION	NOTES	DATE COMPLETED
Tables are clear, user friendly, and formatted according to the writing style of your field		
Figures are clear, user friendly, and formatted according to the writing style of your field		
Figures and tables are reviewed for relevance and value		
Figures and tables are provided in appendices and references in the appropriate place in the body of the chapter		
A summary of findings is provided and leads to the final chapter		

CHAPTER 11

Implications and Conclusion

Congratulations! You're now about to begin writing the final chapter of your dissertation. You have collected your data, analyzed the results, and presented your findings. At this time, your attention turns to providing a discussion of the findings as they relate to the existing literature and the implications this brings for your profession and field. You explore the strengths and weaknesses of your study, suggesting the next logical steps in the research, and provide a conclusion to your dissertation. This chapter serves as a discussion of the application of your finding and a summary of your work.

Writing Your Final Chapter

As you begin to outline your final chapter, you want to consider how to accurately summarize the study, link the findings to the literature, explore the strengths and limitations of the study, and explain the implications of the findings for your profession. Consider recommendations for future research and provide a summary of your work. This chapter will begin by introducing the chapter. Here you summarize your methodology one last time and include an overview of what the reader will find. Be sure to include a brief discussion of the study's problem statement and what the study aimed to answer.

Discussion of Findings

In your last chapter you discussed your findings by reviewing the results. In this final dissertation chapter, you explore these, with a focus on the interpretation of those findings and a discussion exploring the relationship between them and the study's problem and purpose statements. This is accomplished by providing a summary of your study and the major findings. You then link your study results with the prior research from your literature review and any additional information you may have found since. Your discussion will focus on how each of the findings supports the purpose of your study and the body of research on this topic. If your findings challenge the current literature, discuss how and what may attribute to this.

After you have thoroughly explored the implications of your results on the current literature, turn your discussion to focus on how these findings impact your study's population. How do your findings support or contrast the prior literature? Explore the implications: What does each mean as it is applied? What was surprising from your results? Why? How can we apply this to the population at large? Provide a strong summary of this discussion before turning your attention to the next topic of exploration, the implications of your results on your field and profession.

Implications for the Profession

This section of your chapter affords you the opportunity to discuss how your study enhances both the knowledge and skills of your chosen profession. This may be accomplished, similarly to the discussion, by comparing your results with the current literature. Discuss all aspects of how this will benefit the consumer, on all levels, as well as how it will benefit the the field, for example counselors, counselor educators, school administrators on the counselor education level, and the like. Explore what other related fields this may apply to. For instance, if your study was on correctional staff and burnout prevention, they may relate to other first responders such as firefighters, police officers, nurses, sheriffs, and paramedics. This is an opportunity to explore the vast reaches of your results to not only your field but those related to it.

Strengths and Limitations of the Study

In this section of your final chapter, you explore the strengths and limitations of your study. In your methodology chapter, you cited limitations of your study. Review those and discuss any additional limitations that may have developed as the study progressed. Some new limitations may have revealed themselves during your data collection and analysis, but some unforeseen strengths may have appeared as well. This is your opportunity to provide a balanced assessment of your study to the reader.

Suggestions for Future Research

At this juncture, you explore recommendations for future research based on your current results. Take this opportunity to call attention to any unexpected findings or those that challenge the current literature. What would you do differently next time knowing what you know now? If you had unlimited time and resources, what is the best possible way to study these phenomena? Afford yourself this opportunity to explore changes you may have made, or ones you will include in future research. This section allows you to honestly evaluate both your study and the implications of its results on the literature. Provide insights for the next researcher or begin to outline your next research project.

Conclusion of Your Dissertation

Congratulations are in order once again! You have made it to the final section of your dissertation. You want to finish strong as you bring the entire study to a final summary for the reader.

A strong summary will begin at the beginning. Highlight the core areas of your dissertation. If you look back on the major headings in chapters 1, 3, and 4 of your dissertation, you find key topics to include in your conclusion.

Begin with a brief review of the purpose, need, and problem statements of your study. Provide an overview of your research design and how it best targets your research questions. Explain your population by providing details about your participants and sample size, as well as your instrumentation and methodology. Summarize your results a final time as well as the implications of these on both the literature and your field. Conclude this chapter with recommendations for future research, and you are done!

Upon conclusion, you will finalize all your references and appendices. These will include any tables and figures, definitions of terms, and glossaries you may have created. Some programs require you to include your current curriculum vitae as an appendix, so check your dissertation handbook and discuss this with your chair. You are advised not to include your home address or home phone number on this document, as that is not something you want to be published. Other programs require a journal article submission of your dissertation findings. Again, refer to your dissertation handbook and explore this with your chair. If this is required, it will most likely be a draft suitable for submission, so be sure to be aware of this expectation as this may require additional time to complete prior to submitting your final dissertation document.

Double-check all your appendices. These may include such items as your call for participants, the informed consent, any documentation of required ethical training, and your IRB approval notice. Additionally, documentation of permission to use instruments or a copy of your interview will be included as applicable. Your chair and committee may require additional information to be included, so be sure to check with them to ensure all necessary appendices are complete. It is highly recommended that you double-check the order of these according to how they present in your dissertation and that they are consistent with the title for each (i.e., Appendix A in the text is the same Appendix A subject wise).

Summary

The final chapter of your dissertation affords you the opportunity to explore the findings of your study from the vantage point of how they support or challenge the current literature and how they contribute to your field. You have worked long and hard on this project, so do not allow yourself to simply write off this chapter as a summary. Explore the implications of your results for your profession and field, highlighting the contribution you made to the science. Critically evaluate the strengths and weaknesses of your work. Explore the next logical steps of the research and make strong suggestions for what those may be. You have contributed to the field, but this is also your opportunity to help guide future researchers and students, extending the impact of your work.

You began your dissertation with a strong chapter outlining the needs for your study and the questions it aimed to answer. Take your time when constructing your final chapter, allowing for a full exploration of each element. This brings your study to a logical and strong conclusion, one that reflects only your hard work and dedication and introduces you to the world of academia as a researcher. Seize this opportunity to highlight your work and contribution to the field!

Online Resources

Editage.com. (n.d.a.). *Q & A forum: Results and discussion: Q: Can you give me an example of implications of future research?* https://www.editage.com/insights/give-me-an-example-of-impication-for-further-research#:~:text=Research%20implications%20suggest%20how%20the,policy%2C%20practice%2C%20or%20theory

> *Provides a clear explanation and example of how to explain the implications of your findings as they relate to your field.*

Chuah Kee Man. (2020, November 27). *How to write the implications section of research writing.* https://www.youtube.com/watch?v=263PAs7oC_8

> *This short video highlights the importance of implications of research and outlines how to write this section in a research paper.*

Editage.com. (n.d.b.). *Q & A forum: Results and discussion: Q: In research, what is the difference between implication and recommendation?* https://www.editage.com/insights/in-research-what-is-the-difference-between-implication-and-recommendation

> *Provides a discussion distinguishing the implications of research from future recommendations for a research study.*

Worksheet 11.1: Checklist for Writing the Final Chapter of Your Dissertation

ELEMENT OF THE CHAPTER	IMPORTANT POINTS TO INCLUDE FROM THE STUDY	NOTES	COMPLETED
Introduction			
Review of findings as they relate to the literature			
Implications to the literature			
Implications to the profession/field of study			
Strengths of the study			
Limitations of the study			
Suggestions for future research			

CHAPTER 12

Final Defense Preparation

Preparing for your final defense will feel somewhat familiar as it mimics your preparation for your dissertation proposal. Many of the same steps will remain consistent, and fortunately you have already done them, so there will be less confusion. The most significant difference is that now you are presenting the findings of your study.

The Final Defense Process

You have accomplished major milestones in your journey toward your PhD. You have successfully defended your dissertation proposal, gained IRB approval, and both collected and analyzed your data. You have written your final chapters in which you present your findings (Chapter 4) and discussed them along with your study's strengths, limitations, and implications to your chosen field. You have worked alongside your chair in assuring your formatting fits the criteria set for by your institution and gained approval to schedule your final defense, a process that mirrors that outlined in Chapter 8 of this text. As you go into the defense, you need to switch from student to expert of this subject matter. No one knows more about this subject than you. This is a significant paradigm shift.

Contacting Your Committee Members

Contact your committee members using a professional tone, acknowledge their contributions throughout the process, and provide them with a copy of your finished dissertation per your chair's preference and direction. Consider the purpose of contact and allow this to dictate your means of contact. Email is appropriate for providing versions of your chapters but may be inconvenient when scheduling. Your schedule and that of your chair are most important, so provide a few days and times to your committee that fit your schedules.

Scheduling Considerations

When scheduling your proposal defense, consider streamlining the process using such polling websites such as Doodle, Typeform, or Survey Monkey. Use of this platform will make the scheduling of your final defense effective as well. Consideration of time zone differences remains important. Review and discuss these expectations with your chair to ensure compliance with institutional and program expectations. Worksheet 12.1 provides a checklist for considerations when working toward gaining approval from your chair and scheduling your defense with your committee members for your final defense. Discuss with your chair the expectations and rules of the final defense, as well as the opportunity to invite friends and family and what expectations there are for their attendance.

Preparing Your Presentation

Your experience from preparing your proposal defense presentation will assist you in preparing your presentation for your final defense. Timing considerations still need to be considered. The final defense outline may be provided by your department and/or chair, but if not, a general guideline is to provide a brief overview of chapters 1 through 3 and then address the major content areas of chapters 4 and 5. There is no need to spend a lot of time on the literature review or rational for the study; just a brief refresher is necessary. Review your institutional handbook and your completed chapters, making note of your major and secondary headers. These will guide your outline. Most of your time will be spent discussing your hypotheses, results, limitations, delimitations, and implications of the findings to the field.

Since your committee has already read your dissertation and approved chapters 1–3, a brief review of these chapters is appropriate. Provide your committee members with an overview of your study, a summary of the significance of your study, and your problem and purpose statements, along with an overview of the research questions. An overview of your literature review is not necessary at this juncture. A discussion of your methodology, including a discussion of your theoretic lens and conceptual framework, as applicable, along with the research design and interpretive framework used in your data analysis, need to be included, as well as a summary of the chosen population and sampling procedures.

The final defense will focus primarily on your results and findings. You want to provide an overview of your data processing techniques. For qualitative designs this includes a discussion of how you arrived at your themes and constructs. For quantitative designs, this includes a discussion of the statistical analysis performed and significant information regarding demographics, sample size, and the handling of missing data.

The discussion of your findings will depend on the nature of your study. For qualitative designs, you want to report how these themes and constructs align with or challenge the prior literature and explain how each contributes to the implications of this study. For quantitative studies, discuss each hypothesis and how your findings provides support or challenge the purpose of the study, the prior literature, your hypotheses, and the statistical significance and how each contributes to the implications of this study.

Identify and discuss the limitations and discuss suggestions for future research as well. Consider what you would do differently, spotlight any surprising findings, and discuss the next logical steps in the research to further explore your topic. Finally, provide a personal reflection where you discuss what this process was like for you and what you learned from it.

You may want to consider reviewing your prior drafts and the feedback or questions posed by your chair and committee. As recommended when preparing for your proposal defense, reviewing these as you prepare for your dissertation will assist you in targeting prior areas in your presentation. Attending or viewing completed dissertation defenses from your department, if available, or on the internet, can provide you with a sense of the final defense tone and format.

The timing of your presentation continues to be imperative. They are determined by your program, so presentation times will vary, and understanding that expectation is important in your presentation preparation. It is again highly recommended that you practice the timing of your presentation prior to your final defense so that you are confident in presenting the information in a thorough and complete way without feeling rushed or being cut off due to time limitations. Worksheet 12.2 provides a checklist to assist you in preparing for your final dissertation defense.

The Final Defense Day

Your final defense day has arrived. Remember that helpful checklist, which includes double-checking your technology, including your internet connection if presenting from a distance and the share-screen process of your online platform. If presenting in person, double-checking your technology for your presentation is necessary to ensure it's working correctly and that your presentation can be viewed clearly by your committee members. Use your prior experience with your proposal defense to calm your nerves and allow you to enjoy this significant event.

Prepare yourself once again in professional attire and ensure that if presenting remotely that your background and seating is professional as well. Approach this with professionalism as an expectation as this is the final step toward completing your dissertation and earning your PhD. This is serves as the bridge from PhD candidate to PhD. Review any questions you were asked at your proposal or that came up through the revisions of your final chapters. Confirm with your chair that they will take notes during the questions and provide you with any adjustments and feedback from the committee upon completion.

Prior to the start of your defense, take a deep breath and enjoy this moment, as it is most likely the only time in your life your will defend a dissertation. This is a significant step in your dissertation process and your journey to becoming a PhD. Approach this day as one of accomplishment, one you are confident in your preparation for; remember, your committee wants you to do well.

The Final Defense and Considerations

All of your hard work is coming to a final presentation. Consider the etiquette of the setting as you did in your proposal defense. If presenting in person or remotely, be sure to acknowledge each of your committee members and thank them for attending and their work on your research. Your chair will most likely begin the final defense by thanking the committee for attending and then transfer the discussion to you to begin your presentation. Present your information as you have practiced it, professionally and at a pace that allows you to work within the time restrictions but doesn't seem rushed. Upon completion, open the presentation to questions from your committee.

Keep in mind that questions from your committee occur for various reasons. Field these questions as inquiries and answer each to the best of your ability in a professional and respectful tone, asking for clarification of the question if necessary. Answer questions concisely and be aware of your tone. Don't allow it to become defensive or abrasive because you are uncomfortable; maintain your professionalism as it personifies you as a PhD. Remain focused on the scope of your study. Questions may arise outside that scope, but don't be tempted to respond. Respond only to what you can back up with facts from your findings. Acknowledge all other questions, but politely inform your committee that the answers fall outside of the focus of your study, but you would be happy to explore these and get back to them in the future. If they take you up on this, be sure you do.

After all questions have been posed and answered, you will be asked to leave the dissertation defense, as you were in your proposal defense, to allow your committee to discuss their decision and any applicable recommendations. Upon your return, your chair will welcome you back and inform you of the committee's decision.

Possible outcomes include a pass, pass with revision, and a failure consistent with those of the proposal defense. A pass with revisions will consist of adjustments suggested by your committee to enhance, add, or clarify your study. A failure at this point will need to be discussed with your chair after the final defense meeting, as each institution provides different guidelines regarding the steps following this. Receiving a pass indicates that the committee feels your proposal is ready for ProQuest review, if your institution participates in this publication program. Remember to be gracious and thank your committee members for their work and feedback on your study. After celebrating this accomplishment, you will work with your chair to complete your ProQuest application and submit it, a process that is discussed in the following section.

After the Successful Defense

Congratulations! You successfully defended your final defense. You've celebrated this milestone and now need to focus and get back to work to finish the process. The steps this involves varies by institution, so consult your institutional dissertation handbook and discuss these steps with your chair. Minimally, you need to provide your institution with an electronic copy of your finalized dissertation, including a signature sheet. Other institutions require printed copies to be submitted. The finalized versions sometimes also include a completed article of your dissertation for submission to professional journals. Some programs may require your finalized version to be reviewed by an editor prior to submission. Consult your program's handbook to ensure you comply with the expectations.

Your doctoral program may require your finalized dissertation to be submitted to the Cataloging in Publishing (CIP) program of the U.S. Library of Congress. The purpose of this program is "to serve the nation's libraries by cataloging books in advance of publication" (U.S. Library of Congress, n.d.a., para. 1). Once submitted the Library of Congress creates a "bibliographic record for each publication and sends it to the publisher" who "prints the record [known as CIP data] on the verso of the title page" (para. 1). A faculty member at your institution serves as the designated reviewer and provides you with any recommended edits prior to submitting it to the Library of Congress for consideration.

Once you have successfully completed your final submission, you're on your way to becoming a PhD. Keep in mind, this title cannot be used until your degree is conferred, so patience is imperative. Soon enough, graduation will transpire and you, dressed in your regalia, will obtain your diploma and finally be PHinisheD!

Summary

Preparing for your dissertation final defense is a significant moment in your academic career and a milestone in your progression toward completing your PhD. It is different from your proposal defense, but you are already familiar with the general format and process. Continuing to work closely with your chair throughout chapter revisions and the finalization of your appendices is imperative. Your program's dissertation guide will provide invaluable information on the required content and format.

Preparation for your final defense begins with your five chapters and related appendices, which provide the foundation for your presentation. Your graduate dissertation handbook will outline proposal defense specifics regarding format and time restrictions. You'll provide a brief overview of the study's significance, your problem and purpose statements, and an overview of the research questions, as your committee has already approved this information. An overview of your literature review is not necessary. A discussion of your methodology, the research design, data analysis procedures, and interpretive framework needs to be included, as well as a summary of the chosen population and sampling procedures. A discussion of your findings will depend on the nature of your study. A thorough discussion of the implication and recommendations these results have for your chosen field, as well as that of the study's limitations, will be expected. Suggestions for the future and a personal reflection will complete your presentation.

The day of your final defense is a momentous occasion, one you need to approach with professionalism but also savor. After successfully defending your dissertation, your next major task will be to comply with your department's requirements to finish the dissertation process, which may require submitting copies to application to the CIP program. After you have completed these steps, you are finally PHinisheD, but wait until graduation to use that new title.

Online Resources

Jansen, D., & Phair, D. (2021, June). *Preparing for your dissertation defence: 13 key questions you need to be ready for.* https://gradcoach.com/dissertation-thesis-defence/

> Provides a list of questions for consideration prior to your dissertation.

Lantsoght, E. (2017, February). How to prepare for your PhD defense [Blog post]. *Academic Transfer.* https://www.academictransfer.com/en/blog/how-to-prepare-for-your-phd-defense/

> Provides helpful hints to prepare for your final defense.

U.S. Library of Congress. (n.d.). *About CIP.* https://www.loc.gov/publish/cip/about/process.html

> A useful outline of the application process for submitting dissertations to the U.S. Library of Congress.

Watson, C. (2020, August). *The dissertation defense guide.* https://mydissertationeditor.com/dissertation-defense/

> *Helpful guide on various topics related to the dissertation, ranging from choice of outfits, possible questions, to an overview of the dissertation process.*

Reference

U.S. Library of Congress. (n.d.). *About CIP.* https://www.loc.gov/publish/cip/about/process.html

Worksheet 12.1: Checklist for the Final Defense Process

CONSIDERATION	STEPS TAKEN TO ACCOMPLISH THIS		DATE COMPLETED
Gaining approval for your proposal from your chair	Provided finalized versions of chapters 1–5 with all appendices to your chair for review		
	Gained final approval of chapters 1–5 with all appendices from your chair		
	Discussed timeframe of final defense with chair, completed any necessary paperwork to obtain this per your institutional requirements (i.e., dissertation proposal topic approval; dissertation proposal date approval, etc.)		
	Agreed on workable final defense date range with chair		
Contacting your committee	Discuss with chair who will contact the committee members re: final defense date		
	If dissertation chair is contacting committee members	Provide dates/times and any additional details to chair	
	If you are responsible for contacting committee members	Choose method of contact	
		Provide a range of dates and times available for the proposal	
		Confirm chosen date that works for all committee members	
		Send notice of location of defense or platform link if defending remotely	

Worksheet 12.2: Important Items to Include in Your Presentation

ITEM	INFORMATION TO INCLUDE	SLIDE NUMBER OF PRESENTATION
Brief overview of study		
Significance of study		
Problem statement		
Purpose statement		
Brief review of research questions		
Methodology discussion overview		
Brief review of research design		
Review of interpretive framework		
Brief overview of population and inclusion/exclusion criteria		
Brief summary of sampling procedures		
Discussion of data processing		
Discussion of findings: • Each hypothesis and how your findings relate to the literature (support or challenge) • How each provides support for or challenges the purpose of the study and the prior literature and how each contributes to the implications of the study		
Discussion of implications and recommendations to your chosen field/profession		
Identification and discussion of limitations of your study • Noting strengths can provide balance		

(continued)

ITEM	INFORMATION TO INCLUDE	SLIDE NUMBER OF PRESENTATION
Discussion of suggestions for future research • What you would do differently • Any surprising findings • Next logical steps in the research to further explore your topic		
Personal reflection • What the process like for you, what you learned from it		
Conclusion		
Discussion opened to your committee for questions		

CHAPTER 13

Publication and Your Article

You've completed your dissertation defense and submitted all your paperwork. You're now a PhD and ready to move forward with the next phase of your dissertation study: publication of the study and development of an article on the results. This process may be part of your program's expectations, or it may be something you choose to pursue on your own. You have completed a significant amount of work and have found important information adding to the literature of your field. Now is the time to disseminate this information through publication of both your dissertation and an article summarizing the study and findings.

After Your Dissertation

It is recommended that you explore your program's expectations regarding the publication of your dissertation or the related article. Some programs will require this and provide a review prior to submitting your dissertation to a publication system such as ProQuest. Others may require an outline of your article as part of your completed dissertation but not require follow-through of submission. Others simply require the filing of your completed dissertation within the department or school. Regardless of the expectation, you are encouraged to explore publication opportunities for both your dissertation and its related article with your chair. The dissemination of results is an important aspect of research, which will bring your study full circle.

Publication of Your Dissertation

Exploring the opportunities to publish your dissertation begins with a discussion with your chair and review of the expectations of your program's dissertation handbook. ProQuest is often used as the publication service for dissertations: "As the official repository of the Library of Congress, PQDT Global provides researchers with quality and equitable search results across all institutions, as well as rich citation data that delivers insights into the connections building around the world" (ProQuest, n.d.c., para. 2).

Both the researcher and institution benefit from publications of dissertations. Most significantly for you, publication assists in developing "a reputable historical foundation of research for your topic" (ProQuest, n.d.b., para. 1). Additionally, publication with ProQuest makes your dissertation available to academic databases and Google Scholar, thereby making your results available to your peers and students alike (ProQuest, n.d.b.). Questions regarding the ownership of your dissertation are clarified by ProQuest (n.d.b.):

> The copyright of the dissertation is held by the author. The author grants ProQuest the "license" – i.e. the right to display the dissertation on the ProQuest platform. The license is non-exclusive: the author has full authorization to publish a book or to have the dissertation available on another website. (para. 13)

This helps in assuring your academic work remains yours but is available to other scholars and students alike.

Throughout this process you want to work closely with your chair and department if your program requires publication as part of your dissertation process. If this is not a requirement for your dissertation but something you want to explore, it is highly recommended you discuss this with your chair and explore the ProQuest site for details of the process. You need to have the support and assistance of your chair during the submission process regardless of the departmental expectations should you plan to pursue this publication opportunity.

Transitioning Your Dissertation to an Article

Another wonderful publication opportunity is that of an article rooted in your dissertation. This is not just a condensed version of your dissertation but an article presenting your findings in a peer-reviewed journal dedicated to your field of study. This transition involves both time and dedication and often occurs after graduation has been commenced and you have more time to settle into your role as a PhD.

Specific publishers will have different expectations regarding the manuscript formatting and length as well as details that need to be included. You are encouraged to explore various journals in your field and investigate their topic focus to determine if your article will fit the publisher's central theme. Also, explore their proposal policy, which will outline when documents are accepted, the submission process, and the expected format. Plan for critiques and revisions throughout this process like when writing your dissertation. This is intended to provide you with constructive feedback to strengthen and clarify your article and is part of the process.

The American Psychological Association (APA) provides a great resource for turning your dissertation into an article. They recommend reviewing previously published articles in journals to which you are considering submitting your article to gain insights into the type of subjects they include as well as the formatting requested (APA, n.d.). Also, consider the due dates for submissions, as some publications have open acceptance windows while others have strict due dates for proposals. It's also recommended to discuss these requirements with your chair and work with them on adapting the dissertation to an article submission (APA, n.d.).

The abstract is usually much more concise than that of a dissertation, with limits set forth by various writing styles (APA, n.d.). Steps to transition your dissertation to an article ready for publication include focusing on reducing the length (APA, n.d.); concisely stating the need for the study, problem, and purpose statements; and providing a brief summary of your literature review to provide an understanding of the importance of this study. You also want to summarize your methodology and focus on sharing your results and the implications of the study in a focused manner.

Your results should be concisely summarized, with attention to the connection of these results to your research questions. A clear connection needs to be established for clarity. Your discussion section will be reduced to focusing specifically on how your results support or challenge prior findings while considering your current population, issues, as well as the strengths and limitation of your study's design (APA, n.d.). While this process takes some time, it is a wonderful way to parlay all of your hard work into a second publication.

Submitting Your Article for Publication

Submitting your article for publication is a long process that includes feedback from the journal reviewers as well as redrafts, as needed. You start with working to make your lengthy dissertation more concise and within the page limits set forth by the journal. Focus first on condensing your dissertation to the desired length while keeping the important aspects of the study intact. Only after you have achieved a reduction in length do you begin editing the writing. Attempting to do both at once can be overwhelming and result in incomplete thoughts. Have others read your article prior to submission, as you did with your dissertation. When you are working so closely with a subject sometimes the words on the page are not accurate reflections of what you intended to say. Use your peers to assist with this, especially those who have gone through the dissertation process themselves. They will understand the importance of feedback and editing and be able to provide helpful feedback.

Do your research on the journals you are considering submitting your article to. What is their focus? A journal designed for counselor educators will want an article to tie into that population's needs and focus. One focusing on engineering will want your article to relate to issues relevant to that profession. Explore their expectations regarding length and formatting. Do they expect a certain number of pages or words? Will they be using APA formatting or MLA, or perhaps some other writing style specific to any given profession? What are the due dates for submissions, and when can you expect to receive feedback on your article? Ensure you follow the correct submission procedures, so be sure to read and follow the directions provided by the journal editors to avoid misunderstandings or loss of your submission (*The Guardian*, n.d., para. 13).

Be prepared for feedback. Unlike your dissertation, these reviews will most likely be completed by people unknown to you. This feedback may not be packaged as it was from your dissertation chair or committee members. It may be quite direct or rather vague. It may mesh personal preferences and opinions with constructive feedback. You will need to be sure to take a deep breath and try to be as objective as you can when reading the feedback, as it can sometimes come across a bit differently and be somewhat difficult to accept on a work you spent so much time on. Remember, this is constructive feedback regardless of the packaging, so sift through it and be able to acknowledge that which will polish and strengthen this article version of your study. Incorporate the feedback and resubmit your article; this is normal in the process, so don't view this as a failure or give up on your goal (*The Guardian*, n.d.). You worked hard on your dissertation and will need to put the same effort forth in this process, so be sure to dedicate time to this process.

Summary

Publishing your study may or may not be a step in your program's dissertation process. If this is expected, be sure to consult with your chair and gain guidance through this process. If it is not, explore this option with your chair outside of the program's expectations. Publication of your results is an important step in both disseminating your results as well as gaining additional acknowledgement of your work.

Transitioning your dissertation into an article ready for publication in a professional journal is a logical step. You can parlay your work from your dissertation into a second publication, which benefits you tremendously within academia by increasing the dissemination of your research results. This process is not one that occurs easily, but it is realistically accomplishable.

Completion of your dissertation defense is only one step of you becoming a PhD. Your dissertation is your introduction to academia that provides an evaluation of your expertise within your field while the subsequent article is your introduction to consumers within your field. Publishing both your dissertation and possibly an article summarizing your study transitions you from researcher to academic contributor. Both of these roles are underpinning of the true Doctor of Philosophy and ones to embrace.

Online Resources

American Psychological Association. (n.d.). *Adapting a dissertation or thesis into an article*. https://apastyle.apa.org/style-grammar-guidelines/research-publication/dissertation-thesis

> *Provides a great guide in turning your dissertation into an article.*

F1000Research. (n.d.). *How to publish: Submit your research*. https://f1000research.com/for-authors/publish-your-research

> *Provides a great checklist of seven considerations prior to submission of an article for any publication.*

The Guardian. (n.d.). How to get published in an academic journal: top tips from editors: Journal editors share their advice on how to structure a paper, write a cover letter—and deal with awkward feedback from reviewers. https://www.theguardian.com/education/2015/jan/03/how-to-get-published-in-an-academic-journal-top-tips-from-editors

> *Provides constructive insights into what publishers are looking for in an article submission and great advice on how to separate feedback from opinion and use it constructively.*

Masterclass. (2021, September 7). How to get an article published in a magazine in 5 steps. https://www.masterclass.com/articles/how-to-get-an-article-published-in-a-magazine

> *Although not specific to dissertation articles, this site provides an overview of steps to get an article published and provides helpful hints.*

Mesquita, L. (2018, March 22). *Eight top tips to help you turn your PhD thesis into an article: Sharing insights from the latest Researcher Academy webinar.* Elsevier Connect. https://www.elsevier.com/connect/authors-update/eight-top-tips-to-help-you-turn-your-phd-thesis-into-an-article

Moss, L. (2019, May 15). *25 ways to increase your chances at publication: Successful articles share certain elements, writes Laura Moss, an editor of a scholarly journal who's written hundreds of decision letters.* Inside Higher Ed. https://www.insidehighered.com/advice/2019/05/15/how-increase-your-chances-getting-your-work-published-scholarly-journal-opinion

Provides insights on how decision are made on article submissions and helpful hints to include in yours.

ProQuest. (n.d.). *Dissertations & theses.* https://about.proquest.com/en/dissertations/

Provides an overview of the dissertation publication process as well as the benefits of publication.

References

American Psychological Association. (n.d.). Adapting a dissertation or thesis into a journal article. https://apastyle.apa.org/style-grammar-guidelines/research-publication/dissertation-thesis

The Guardian. (n.d.). How to get published in an academic journal: Top tips from editors: Journal editors share their advice on how to structure a paper, write a cover letter—and deal with awkward feedback from reviewers. https://www.theguardian.com/education/2015/jan/03/how-to-get-published-in-an-academic-journal-top-tips-from-editors

ProQuest. (n.d.a). *Benefits for researchers.* https://about.proquest.com/en/products-services/pqdtglobal

ProQuest. (n.d.b). *Frequently asked questions.* https://about.proquest.com/en/dissertations/proquest-dissertations-frequently-asked-questions/proquest-dissertations-authors-frequently-asked-questions/

ProQuest. (n.d.c). *ProQuest: The world leader in dissertation access and dissemination.* https://about.proquest.com/en/dissertations/

Worksheet 13.1: Exploring Professional Journals for Publication Checklist

JOURNAL EXPECTATION	NOTES
What is the journal topic focus?	
Who is the readership?	
What is the writing style?	
What is the page length?	
What are the expectations of the title page?	
What are the specifics of the abstract?	
What are the expectations regarding references?	
What file format does the submission need to be in?	
What are the timelines expected by the publisher for submissions and versions?	
What is the review process?	
How is feedback provided?	
How will you be notified of the final decision regarding the article's acceptance or denial?	

Glossary

Annotated bibliography a document is comprised of a list of references followed by an annotation of the work, or a summary statement of the major points and thoughts presented (American Psychological Association [APA], 2020). Stated differently, it is a document containing the full citation of articles or books, followed by a detailed evaluation of the literature. These often include a summary of the study, methodology, results, and critical assessment of the application of the article to the subject you are researching.

Annotations Summary statements of major points/thoughts.

Approach to inquiry The particular qualitative genre of the study.

Assumptions What you believe to be true but can't support with the prior literature/science.

Audit trail A document detailing the route a researcher took to arrive at the findings of the study.

Axiology A qualitative assumption that believes all research is heavily loaded with the values and value system of the inquirer, the theory, the paradigm used, and the social and cultural norms of the inquirer and respondents. These values are acknowledged and discussed in the research.

Between group (between-subject) designs Sometimes called comparative designs, they "compare between different treatment groups and/or with control groups" (Heppner et al., 2016, p. 245).

Categorical variables Vary in nature such as people, places, or things.

Causal comparative designs Identify the effects of naturally occurring variables ex post facto, after the fact (Houser, 2020).

Characterological variable Represents varying degrees of participant maturation.

Cohorts Common and naturally occurring nonequivalent groups. They represent existing and nonrandom groups within applied settings that have similar conditions.

Comparison group Study participants who receive an alternative treatment or intervention that the researcher compares to the treatment provided to the experimental group (Houser, 2020).

Conceptual framework "The overarching argument for the work—both why it is worth doing and how it should be done" (Ravitch & Riggan, 2017, p. 8) that "incorporates pieces that are borrowed from elsewhere, but the structure, the overall coherence, is something that you build, not something that exists ready-made" (Maxwell, 2005, p. 41).

Confounding variables Often exist outside of the parameters of the study but might influence the variables of interest indirectly.

Constant comparative method Refers to the researcher constantly comparing incidents, events, and activities identified in the research to an emerging category with the hopes of developing and saturating the category.

Construct The variable or concept you are exploring in your study.

Continuous variables Values that fall along a numerical continuum and are not limited to specific numerical values (McBurney & White, 2004; Tabachnick & Fidell, 2019).

Control group Study participants who do not receive a treatment.

Control (covariate) variables A unique type of independent variable that can potentially influence the dependent variable.

Correlational descriptive designs Seek to identify and understand the associations among variables through inferential statistics (Houser, 2020; McGregor, 2018).

Counterbalanced crossover design Attempts to control for the order of exposure to interventions. The instrumentation researchers utilize in a counterbalanced crossover design include a pretest, a measure when the groups change treatments, and a measurement at the end of treatment or posttest.

Criterion sampling Involves the researcher identifying specific and important criterion that participants must meet for participation in the study.

Crossover design Requires participants to switch from one experimental condition to another, representing two independent variables, at a specified time in the study. Objective observations and instrumentation during the course study measure the changes by the various treatments.

Culture/cultural group Culture is the way of life for a group of people that can be passed down from generation to generation. It can be seen in the behaviors, language, and artifacts of the group.

Delimitations The intentional choices made by the researcher that indicate how you have chosen to narrow the scope of their study.

Dependent samples experiment Assigns participants to groups randomly per an assumption about a variable that researchers want to account for in the study.

Dependent variables Connote the measurable outcomes.

Descriptive problems Illuminate naturally occurring phenomena within a specific population that would benefit from further study because of limited knowledge, theory, or research.

Descriptive theory Articulates the characteristics of the phenomena and the key variables that influence it.

Difference problems Investigate the dissimilarities among two or more phenomena of interest.

Discrete variables Represent categories of finite and small values that are organized by rank or the representation of the value of distinct occurrences (Tabachnick & Fidell, 2019).

Discriminant sampling A form of sampling that occurs late in grounded theory after the researcher has developed a model to determine if the model will remain relevant if more information is gathered on individuals similar to those initially interviewed. To verify the model, the researcher selects sites, people, and/or documents that will expand the storyline, highlights the connections between categories, and fills in information for categories that are not fully developed.

Doctoral comprehensive examination An examination to establish that a doctoral student has successfully transitioned from doctoral student to doctoral candidate. The comprehensive examinations are design to establish the candidate's ability to synthesize the various core areas of their field and comprehensively explain information in both written and oral formats. A passing score promotes a doctoral student to doctoral candidate and allows them to proceed with the dissertation.

Epistemological perspective May also be referred to as the researcher's interpretive framework (e.g., social constructivism, pragmatism, etc.).

Epistemology A philosophical assumption of qualitative research that refers to beliefs about knowledge and how knowledge is constructed. It addresses the relationship between the researcher and what is being researched.

Epoche (or bracketing) The initial step in "phenomenological reduction" whereby the researcher begins with a clean slate (putting aside all preconceived experiences as best as humanly possible) to fully understand the experiences of the participants of the study.

Experimental designs Often referred to as *true* experimental designs, indicate that a researcher wants to investigate treatments or interventions through the application of scientific methods (e.g., testing a hypothesis; Houser, 2020).

Explanatory theory Finds and accounts for causal relationships.

Exploratory theory Tests or pilots a new method or instrument.

External validity Establishes the scope of applicability of the study results to the real world related to the conditions of study such as population, treatment, outcomes, and settings (Heppner et al., 2016).

Factorial designs May or may not use a control group but do simultaneously study two or more independent variables and their interactive effects on a dependent variable (Heppner et al., 2016).

Focus group interview Qualitative interviews conducted as a group.

Hypothesis What you believe the results will be based on the most recent literature.

Independent variables Represent characteristics that affect outcomes.

Informed consent Permission granted by a research participant indicating that they understand the purpose of the research as well as any possible risks, benefits, and compensation for their participation.

Institutional review board (IRB) "A group that has been formally designated to review and monitor biomedical research involving human subjects. In accordance with FDA regulations, an IRB has the authority to approve, require modifications in (to secure approval), or disapprove research. This group review serves an important role in the protection of the rights and welfare of human research subjects" (U.S. Food and Drug Administration, n.d., para. 1).

Instrumentation Objective observations that standardize the rules for measuring a phenomenon.

Intact instruments Preexisting self-report inventories, rating scales, or surveys that have been evaluated for validity and reliability.

Internal validity Constitutes the extent to which a researcher can determine causal relationships due to the amount of control of these factors in the study: the selection process of the sample of participants from the target population, the assignment procedures of the sample to groups, and the degree of manipulation of study variables.

Interpretive framework The beliefs that guide the researcher's action when administering a study.

Interrupted time series with nonequivalent dependent variables measures Uses two dependent variables that are measured at pre- and postinterruptions.

Interval and ratio scales of measurement Measure values continuously and not in steps.

Intervening or mediating variables Attributes in the middle of independent and dependent variables that could influence the dependent variable.

Interview protocol (or interview guide) The list of questions asked in an interview, used consistently with all participants in the same order and same wording.

Life stories/life histories Narrative is a qualitative approach that focuses on the "lived and told stories of individuals" (Creswell & Poth, 2018, p. 67).

Limitations Restrictions of the design and methodology, such as dependability or generalization, and how you will manage/overcome these, as well as a discussion of any personal biases you have that may impact the study and how you will manage these.

Literature search summary A discussion of how you completed your literature search for your research, including what library databases or search engines you used and what terms (or combination of terms) you searched.

Lived experiences A term used in phenomenological studies that affirms the significance of people's individual experiences as conscious human beings.

Methodological congruence This describes the cohesive nature of a study's purpose, questions, and method, which should be interconnected and interrelated.

Methodology The process and language of research.

Moderating variables Other independent variables that affect either the direction or strength of the relationship between the independent and dependent variables of interest.

Modified instruments Preexisting self-report inventories, rating scales, or surveys that were changed to measure another phenomenon of interest (Creswell, 2014).

Nature of the study The discussion of your chosen design and the rationale for this choice, including a summary of the key concepts of the study and concisely present the methodology.

Need for the study Calling on current literature to provide the rationale for your study.

Nominal scales of measurement Classify objects or events into categorical variables by assigning numbers to represent variations within observations (McBurney & White, 2004).

Nonequivalent groups designs "Comparisons are made between or among groups in non-randomly formed, often pre-existing groups" (Heppner et al., 2016, p. 270).

Nonexperimental or descriptive designs "Describe characteristics or the effects of events for an identified population" (Houser, 2020, p. 58).

Nonprobability sampling methods Participants of the study are drawn from a readily accessible population and based on a specific study criterion.

Observational descriptive designs Attempt to describe behaviors of interest within a specific groups through the objective observation of others or raters (Houser, 2020).

Ontology A branch of philosophy that deals with the nature of reality (truth). Specifically, ontology studies the nature of human beings while looking through the lens of their existence as an individual, in society, and in the universe.

Operational definitions "A detailed specification of how one would go about measuring a given variable. Operational definitions can range from very simple and straightforward to quite complex, depending on the nature of the variable and the needs of the researcher. Operational definitions should be tied to the theoretical constructs under study. The theory behind the research often clarifies the nature of the variables involved and, therefore, would guide the development of operational definitions that would tap the critical variables" (Graziano & Raulin, 2020, para. 1).

Ordinal scales of measurement Organization of objects or events in order of importance or magnitude along a continuum.

Participant observer This is when the researcher participates in the activity at the site and records the data during the activity. They can give the receiver insider views and subjective data.

Participant recruitment The procedures that will be used to solicit or invite potential participants to participate in the study, which may involve activities such as distributing flyers advertising the study, sending emails to electronic mailing lists, or sharing the invitation through professional contacts or organizations.

Phenomenon The central concept being examined by the phenomenologist and being experienced by subjects in a study (e.g., grief, anger, love).

Post hoc statistical power analysis When the researcher calculates the probability of rejecting a false null hypothesis after data collection using the actual sample size (Houser, 2020).

Posttest-only control group design Means that the objective measure is administered after the treatment

Pretest-posttest control group designs Indicate that variables are measured before and after the intervention.

Probability sampling procedures All members of the target population have an equally random chance to participate in the study.

Problem statement A statement of the issue(s) you plan to explore, supported by the recent literature showing the importance of this to your field.

Proxy pretest measure Sensitizing participants to the experimental intervention, through the administration of similar but different pretest dependent variable (Heppner et al., 2016).

Purpose statement A statement of the goal of the research summarizing what it is you are aiming to answer and how it will benefit the stakeholders of your field.

Purposeful sampling (or purposive sampling) The primary sampling approach used in qualitative research. The inquirer specifically selects individuals and sites for the study based on whether they can inform an understanding of the research problem and central phenomenon of the study.

Quantitative research Involves describing, predicting, controlling, or explaining causal connections or noncausal associations through the application of scientific methods.

Quasi-experimental designs Another type of quantitative research that provides researchers with similar benefits of *true experimental* designs, while using study participants who are in existing groups or those who are not randomly assigned to groups (Houser, 2020; McGregor, 2018).

Reflexivity The process of seeking feedback from participants through member checking, ensuring prolonged engagement with participants and persistent observation in the field, and collaborating with participants throughout the study, enabling external audits from a consultant or auditor, generating rich and thick descriptions of participants and the setting, and participating in a peer review or debriefing of the data and research process. Researchers should engage in at least two of the validation strategies, with some being more cost-effective and easier to implement than others (Creswell, 2016).

Relational problems Examine the association between variables.

Relational theory Identifies and explains relationships between variables.

Reliability Consistency and stability of scores over time.

Research paradigm "A research paradigm is a model or approach to research that is considered the standard by a substantial number of researchers in the field based on having been both verified and practiced for a long period of time" (Editages.com, n.d).

Research problem Represents the identified issue a study intends to address.

Research questions The questions you aim to answer through your study.

Researcher-developed instruments Self-report inventories, rating scales, or surveys designed by the research to use in the current study.

Researcher's positionality This term highlights the idea that as researchers we cannot escape the social world we live in to study it. All decisions made by the researcher may be influenced by their position in society and the ideology they believe in.

Response rates The percentage of a target population who respond to a survey.

Sampling methods The procedures to identify and secure people to participate in a research study (Houser, 2020).

Saturation The process of saturating each of the categories with as many incidents, events, or activities as possible to provide support for the categories. This occurs during the data analysis phase of grounded theory. The categories are considered saturated when the researcher cannot find any new information to add to the understanding of the categories.

Scope and delimitations A discussion of the specific focus of your questions and why you chose them, providing an explanation of why are they important to the field.

Secondary pretest design Utilizes the standard pretest-posttest procedures with an additional pretest measure to increase the interpretability of results (Heppner et al., 2016).

Seminal works "Seminal works, sometimes called pivotal or landmark studies, are articles that initially presented an idea of great importance or influence within a particular discipline. Seminal articles are referred to time and time again in the research, so you are likely to see these sources frequently cited in other journal articles, books, dissertations, etc." (North Central University Library, n.d., para. 1).

Significance of the study The discussion of the topic of your research, the importance and value of your study, and the impact this will have on the field and key stakeholders.

Simple-interrupted time series Measures the same number of pre- and postinterruptions of study participants

Snowball sampling A technique used to recruit more research participants by asking the current participants to recommend other potential individuals. This technique is especially useful when the research topic is sensitive or personal. Extra care and consideration should be applied to protect the subjects' privacy.

Statistical power analysis The probability that the selected statistical analysis will result in a rejection of the null hypothesis based on sample size, level of significance, direction of hypothesis testing, and effect size (Houser, 2020).

Survey designs Use self-reports to describe, explain, or explore facts, opinions, behaviors, attitudes, perceptions, and beliefs as well as the relationship among these factors within a target population (Heppner et al., 2016; Houser, 2020). The respondent in survey designs is often from the target population and likely experiences the phenomena of interest.

Temporal order The presented sequence of variables that reflects the probability of effect of one variable on another, which informs the formulation of predictions.

Theoretic framework or lens "Theoretical frameworks provide a particular perspective, or lens, through which to examine a topic. There are many different lenses, such as psychological theories, social theories, organizational theories and economic theories, which may be used to define concepts and explain phenomena" (North Central University Library, n.d., para. 1).

Theoretical sampling A process that begins with homogeneous sample of individuals based on their contribution to the development of the theory, and as the data collection proceeds, categories emerge that allow the researcher to turn to a heterogeneous sample to evaluate if the categories still hold true. Said differently, it is a discussion that explores the foundational concepts and phenomenon of your study, which concisely summarize the conceptual framework derived from the literature.

Thick descriptions Comprehensive descriptions and interpretations of participants or their experiences.

Validity Refers to type of significant and valuable conclusions from the scores.

Variable "Variables represent the measurable traits that can change over the course of a scientific experiment. In all there are six basic variable types: dependent, independent, intervening, moderator, controlled and extraneous variables (Sciencing, 2018).

> An *independent variable* is the cause, or the thing that brings about change, such as an intervention, while the *dependent variable* is the effect, or the thing that changes, such as a decrease in symptoms.
>
> An *intervening variable* is one that impacts the relationship between an independent and dependent variable, such as calories eaten for the independent variable of exercise and the dependent variable of weight.
>
> A *moderator variable* is one [that] impacts the directions and strength of change such as socioeconomic level or age.
>
> *Controlled variables* are those held consistent throughout an experiment, such as an individual's height when measuring changes in body mass index, while *extraneous variables* are those variables not being researched in the current study that may impact the outcome and may lead to an incorrect assumption regarding the relationship between the independent and dependent variables, such as genetic disposition for weight loss.

Within-subject experimental designs Researchers expose participants to all treatment conditions and participants serve as their own control.

Index

A

abstract, 7, 143
American Psychological Association (APA), 13, 91, 93, 142–143
analysis of data. *See* data analysis
annotated bibliography, 13–14, 16, 27, 31
annotations, 13
appendix/appendices, 129
    curriculum vitae as, 129
    double-checking, 129
approach to inquiry, 46
approval for proposal, 100–101
article
    submission for publication, 143–144
    transitioning dissertation to, 142–143
assumptions, 25
audit trail, 57
axiology, 45, 66

B

between-group or between-subject designs, 69
Billups, F. D., 44–45, 50, 52, 55
Bloomberg, L. D., 58
bracketing. *See* epoche/bracketing

C

call for participants, 28, 129
    data collection, 112
    methodology, 86–87, 92–93
case study, 48
Cataloging in Publishing (CIP) program, 135
categorical variables, 68
causal comparative designs, 74
central question, 53
chair, dissertation, 4–5
    approval for proposal, 100–101
characterological variable, 72
Charmaz, K., 49, 56
coding, 56
cohorts, 72
Collaborative Institutional Training Initiative (CITI) training, 99
committee/committee members, 4–6
    contacting, 101, 132
comparison group, 69
compensation, 93, 99–100. *See also* informed consent
conceptual framework, 33, 46, 50–51
conclusion, 128–129
confounding variables, 68
constant comparative method, 49
construct, 14–15, 27, 34–35, 65–67
continuous variables, 68
control group, 69
control (covariate) variables, 68, 71, 91, 114
copyright/copyrighting, 6–7
correlational descriptive designs, 74
counterbalanced crossover design, 70
covariate variables. *See* control (covariate) variables
credibility, 29
Creswell, J. W., 44–47, 49, 51–53, 57, 61, 66–67, 69, 75–76, 78–79
criterion sampling, 54
crossover design, 70
cultural group, 48–49

D

data analysis, 28–29
    presentation, 120–121
    qualitative, 120–121
    quantitative, 121
data collection, 112–115
    call for participants, 112
    demographics, 112–113
    gathering, 28, 113
    informed consent, 113. *See also* informed consent
data processing, 113–114
delimitations
    qualitative methodology, 58
    quantitative methodology, 80
    scope and, 25–26
demographics, 112–113. *See also* data collection
dependent samples experiment, 69

dependent variables, 68
descriptive designs
   correlational, 74
   nonexperimental, 73–74
   observational, 73
descriptive phenomenology, 47
descriptive problems, 75
descriptive theory, 67
difference problems, 75
discrete variables, 68
discriminant sampling, 49
discussion of findings, 127–128
dissertation, 2–8
   process, 22–23
"Dissertation Seminar," 2
doctoral comprehensive examination, 2

E
email, 94, 100–101, 113, 132
epistemological perspective. *See* interpretive framework
epistemology, 45, 66
epoche/bracketing, 47
ethical considerations
   methodology, 91–92
   qualitative methodology, 57–58
   quantitative methodology, 80
ethnography, 48–49
experimental designs, 69–71
explanatory theory, 67
exploratory theory, 67
external validity, 29, 57, 68–73, 79–80, 92

F
factorial designs, 69
feedback, 4–6, 22–23, 57, 98, 100–105, 134, 142–144
final chapter, 127–130
   discussion of findings, 127–128
   implications for profession, 128
final defense, 132–137
   contacting committee members, 132
   presentation, 133–135
   scheduling considerations, 133
findings, discussion of, 127–128
focus group interview, 55
formatting, 122
future research, recommendations for, 128–129

G
Gelinas, L., 54
Google Scholar, 142
grammar and spelling, 35
Grammarly, 36

grounded theory, 49
Guba, E. G., 55, 57

H
Harvard University Graduate School of Arts and Science, 11
Heppner, P. P., 66, 69–71, 73
hermeneutical phenomenology, 47
HHS. *See* U.S. Department of Health and Human Services (HHS)
Houser, R. A., 69, 73, 77
hypothesis, 24, 76, 88–89
hypothesis testing, 76–77, 117, 121

I
independent variables, 67–68
informed consent, 27–29, 87, 89, 91–94, 99–100, 105, 113
institutional review board (IRB), 3–4, 7, 23, 27, 29, 57, 80, 89, 91–94, 99–101, 103–106, 113, 129, 132
instruments/instrumentation, 77–79
   criteria, 78
   descriptors, 78–79
   types, 77–78
intact instruments, 78
internal validity, 29, 57, 68, 70–71, 73, 79–80, 92
interpretative phenomenological analysis (IPA), 48
interpretive framework, 46
interrupted time series with nonequivalent dependent variables, 73
interval and ratio scales, 68
intervening variables, 68. *See also* mediating variables
interview protocol/guide, 55
IPA. *See* interpretative phenomenological analysis (IPA)

L
Library of Congress, 135–136
   Cataloging in Publishing (CIP) program, 135
   PQDT Global, 141–142
life stories/histories, 50
limitations of study, 26, 58, 128
Lincoln, Y. S., 55, 57
literature, 26–27
   reviews, 32–36
   synthesizing, 34–36
literature search summary, 26
lived experience, 44

M
Maxwell, J. A., 51, 53
McBurney, D. H., 66–68, 77
McCaslin, M. L., 46–47

McGregor, S. L. T., 67, 69, 80
mediating variables, 68. *See also* intervening variables
Merriam, S. B., 45, 48, 55–56
methodological congruence, 46, 48, 51, 56, 75
methodologist, 5
methodology, 5–6, 45, 66
    attachments to include, 92–94
    call for participants, 86–87, 92–93
    demographics, 93
    elements, 87–92
    ethical considerations, 91–92
    hypotheses, 88–89
    implementing, 86–87
    informed consent, 93–94
    instrumentation, 89–90
    introduction, 87
    mixed, 6
    participant and sample size, 89
    platform or means of data collection, 94
    qualitative. *See* qualitative research
    quantitative. *See* quantitative research
    research questions, 87–89
    sample and data procedures, 90–91
    statistical analysis, 91
    trustworthiness, 92
moderating variables, 68
Modern Language Association (MLA), 13, 143
modified instruments, 78

N

narrative research, 50
nature of the study, 25
need for the study, 23
nominal scales, 68
nonequivalent groups designs, 71
nonexperimental (descriptive) designs, 73–74
nonprobability sampling methods, 77

O

observational descriptive designs, 73
Office for Human Research Protections, 99, 104
ontology, 45, 66
open-ended questions, 6
operational definitions, 27–28, 34
ordinal scales of measurement, 68

P

participant observer, 49
participant recruitment, 54
participants, 53–54
    call for. *See* call for participants
    compensation, 93, 99–100
    informed consent. *See* informed consent
pass and pass with revisions, 135
    proposal, 103–104

phenomenology, 47–48
phenomenon, 44
population, 27
post hoc statistical power analysis, 79
posttest only control group designs, 70–71
Poth, C. N., 44–47, 49, 51–53, 57, 61
PQDT Global, 141–142
presentation
    considerations, 122
    data analysis, 121–122
    final defense, 133–135
    proposal, 101–103
    qualitive data, 121–122
    quantitative data, 121
    results, 122
pretest-posttest control group designs, 69–71
pretest-posttest designs, 72
probability sampling procedures, 77
problem statement, 24
profession, implications for, 128
proofreading, 35
proposal, 98–106
    contacting committee members, 101
    defense and considerations, 103–104
    gaining approval from chair, 100–101
    IRB requirements, 99–100
    post-successful defense, 104–105
    preparation, 98–99
    presentation, 101–103
    process, 100–102
    scheduling, 101
ProQuest, 135, 141–142
proxy pretest measure, 72
publication, 141–145
    ProQuest, 141–142
    submitting article for, 143–144
purpose statement, 24
purposeful sampling, 45, 53
purposive sampling, 53

Q

qualitative research, 6, 44–60
    case study, 48
    conceptual framework, 46, 50–51
    data analysis presentation, 118–119
    data collection, 53–57
    design and rationale, 50
    ethical considerations, 57–58
    ethnography, 48–49
    goals and purpose, 45
    grounded theory, 49
    interpretive frameworks, 46
    methodological congruence. *See* methodological congruence
    narrative research, 50
    overview, 44–45

phenomenology, 47–48
research problem, 51–52
research purpose statement, 52
research questions, 53
results, example of, 116–117
types, 46–50
quantitative research, 6, 65–81
data analysis presentation, 120
data collection, 79–80
delimitations, 80
elements of, 66
ethical considerations, 80
experimental designs, 69–71
goals and purpose, 66–67
hypotheses, 76
instrumentation, 77–79
limitations, 80
nonexperimental (descriptive) designs, 73–74
overview, 65–66
participants, 76
quasi-experimental designs, 71–73
research design rationale, 69
research problem, 75
research purpose statement, 74–75
research questions, 76
results, example of, 117–119
role of researcher, 79–80
sampling methods, 76–77
theory and variables, 67–68
quasi-experimental designs, 71–73

R

Ravitch, S. M., 51
references, 129
reflexivity, 57
relational problems, 75
relational theory, 67
reliability, 78, 80, 102, 121–122
research design rationale, 69
research paradigm, 24. *See also* qualitative research; quantitative research
research problem, 51–52
research purpose statement
qualitative methodology, 52
quantitative methodology, 74–75
research questions, 24, 53
central question, 53
hypotheses, 88
methodology, 87–88
qualitative methodology, 53
quantitative methodology, 76
sub-questions, 53
researcher-developed instruments, 78

researchers
qualitative research, 55–56
quantitative research, 66, 79–80
researcher's "positionality," 45
response rates, 77
results. *See also* data analysis
presentation, 122
qualitative, example, 116–117
quantitative, example, 117–119
writing, 29–30
Richey, Neil, 11
Riggan, M., 51
role of researcher
qualitative research, 55–56
quantitative research, 66, 79–80
Rubin, H. J., 55
Rubin, I. S., 55

S

sample size justification, 54–55
sampling methods, 76–77
saturation, 55
schedule/scheduling
final defense, 133
proposal defense, 101
scope and delimitations, 25–26
Scott, K. W., 46–47
secondary pretest design, 72–73
seminal works, 13, 34
significance of the study, 23–24
simple-interrupted time series, 73
Smith, J. A., 48
snowball sampling, 54
spelling. *See* grammar and spelling
statistical power analysis, 76
strengths of study, 128
sub-questions, 53
subject matter expert/reader, 5–6
substantive theory, 49
survey designs, 73
synthesizing literature, 34–36

T

temporal order, 67–68
theoretic framework or lens, 25, 33
theoretical sampling, 49
thick description, 49
Tisdell, E. J., 45, 56
title page, 6–7
topics, 11–16
trustworthiness, 56–57
typos and errors, 35

U

U.S. Department of Health and Human Services (HHS), 99, 104

V

validation, 56–57
validity, 29, 56–57, 78, 80–81, 90, 102, 121–122
    external, 29, 57, 68–73, 79–80, 92
    internal, 29, 57, 68, 70–71, 73, 79–80, 92
variables, 12, 34, 67–68
    categorical, 68
    characterological, 72
    confounding, 68
    continuous, 68
    control (covariate), 68, 71, 91, 114
    dependent, 68
    discrete, 68
    independent, 67–68
    intervening, 68
    mediating, 68
    temporal order, 67–68
Volpe, M., 58

W

White, T. L., 66–68, 77
within-subject experimental designs, 70
writing results, 29–30

Y

Yardley, L., 57
Yazan, B., 48
Yin, R. K., 48

About the Authors

Tricia M. Mikolon, PhD, CRC, LPC earned her PhD in counselor education and supervision from Regent University, her master's degree in rehabilitation counseling from the University of Scranton, and her Bachelor of Science degree in psychology from Elizabethtown College. She is a Certified Rehabilitation Counselor and holds an LPC in Pennsylvania as well as board certification in telemental health (BC-TMH). Dr. Mikolon's interests include correctional fatigue, the impact of self-definition and coping skills on holistic recovery, and the use of art therapy techniques in counseling.

She is employed in the Counseling Department at the University of the Cumberlands as an assistant professor and has been on numerous dissertation committees as both chair and committee member. She has instructed in both the master's and doctoral programs while at UC, as well as on both the synchronous and asynchronous platforms, in addition to the traditional classroom. She has authored works on rehabilitation counseling, teaching online, telebehavioral health counseling and supervision, multiculturalism and social justice in counseling, and corrections fatigue. She has presented on the topics of gatekeeping in higher education admissions, multiculturalism and social justice in online teaching, the importance of self-care for counselors, corrections fatigue, motivational interviewing, and co-occurring disorders.

She is an active member of Chi Sigma Iota, the American Counseling Association, The Fraternal Order of Police (Pennsylvania), and Psi Chi. She currently serves as an academic review specialist for the Council for Accreditation of Counseling and Related Educational Programs (CACREP).

Cyrus Williams, PhD, LPC (VA), LMHC (FL), LASPT, CSAT is a full professor and has worked at Regent University for 13 years. Prior to his work at Regent, he worked for more than 15 years in various administrative positions in higher education.

His overall research interest centers on the intersection of ethnicity, social economic status, and education. He focuses on applying non-cognitive variables such as hope, resilience and strength-based interventions to increase access, persistence, retention rates, and the overall college experience for first-generation college students and at-risk individuals and families. Additional research interests include multicultural and advocacy counseling and multicultural competencies and supervision, as well as substance abuse counseling.

In addition to working in higher education, he is the founder and owner of two private practices, Impact Counseling, Coaching, and Consulting and Rapha Counseling Services, Inc., a faith-based counseling center. Dr. Williams is the clinical supervisor and therapist at the private practices. His clinical foci are couples counseling and chemical and sex addiction. Dr. Williams is a trained Gottman Counseling Therapist and an IITAP sex addiction therapist.

In regard to leadership and service to the profession, Dr. Williams is an active member of the American Counseling Association (ACA) and divisions therein (AMCD, AACC, SJ) since 2005. He is an active member and the president of the Virginia Counseling Association, and also served as the president of Virginia Association of Counselor Education and Supervision. Dr. Williams also served as a faculty advisor of Chi Sigma Iota, an international professional and academic counseling honor society, at Regent University and helped students win the Chi Sigma Iota Outstanding Chapter of the Year in 2016.

Dr. Williams has served as the director of the Counselor Education and Supervision Program at Regent University. He teaches in both the Master's in Counseling and Counselor Education and Supervision PhD program.

About the Contributors

Anita M. Pool is an assistant professor in the Department of Counseling at the University of Louisiana at Lafayette, where she teaches the research course to master's-level students. She previously taught qualitative research to doctoral-level students and was the subject matter expert for her department. Pool has also served on numerous dissertation committees as a qualitative methodologist. Additionally, she has presented at several conferences on topics related to qualitative research.

Michell Temple, PhD, EdD, CRC, NCC, CCPT, CTMH, LPC (CO,GA), LPC/MHSP (TN), serves as assistant professor of counseling at Denver Seminary and a private practice rehabilitation and mental health counselor, educator, and supervisor at Temple Renovation Center, LLC. She is a member of the 2019 Cohort of the NBCC-F Mental Health Doctoral Fellowship. She has worked in higher education and community settings. She has published and accepted research on the topics of ethics education in counselor training, rehabilitation counseling, manualized spiritual integrated therapies, and resilience. Temple's research interests include human relationship dynamics, ethics and counselor identity development, resilience, stress, and well-being. She earned a PhD from Regent University in counselor education and supervision and an EdD from the University of West Georgia in Professional Counseling and Supervision. Temple earned a Master of Science in Rehabilitation Counseling from Georgia State University.

www.ingramcontent.com/pod-product-compliance
Lightning Source LLC
Chambersburg PA
CBHW040730020526
44112CB00058B/2910